CATCH
a Falling
Writer

Ruth D. Nelson

Dedicated to my beautiful daughter, Tiffany, for loving me and "my hands" since the moment she was born.

CATCH
a Falling Writer

Connie R. Hebert

CORWIN
A SAGE Company

For information:

Corwin
A SAGE Company
2455 Teller Road
Thousand Oaks,
   California 91320
www.corwinpress.com

SAGE Ltd.
1 Oliver's Yard
55 City Road
London EC1Y 1SP
United Kingdom

SAGE Pvt. Ltd.
B 1/I 1 Mohan Cooperative
   Industrial Area
Mathura Road, New Delhi 110 044
India

SAGE Asia-Pacific Pte. Ltd.
33 Pekin Street #02-01
Far East Square
Singapore 048763

Printed in the United States of America

Library of Congress Cataloging-in-Publication Data

Hebert, Connie R.
Catch a falling writer/Connie R. Hebert.
     p. cm.
Includes bibliographical references and index.
ISBN 978-1-4129-6865-2 (cloth)
ISBN 978-1-4129-6866-9 (pbk.)
    1. English language—Composition and exercises—Study and teaching (Primary) 2. Language arts—Remedial teaching. I. Title.

LB1528.H45 2010
372.62'3—dc22   2009021592

This book is printed on acid-free paper.

09   10   11   12   13   10   9   8   7   6   5   4   3   2   1

Acquisitions Editor:	Jessica Allan
Editorial Assistant:	Joanna Coelho
Production Editor:	Veronica Stapleton
Copy Editor:	Cynthia Long
Typesetter:	C&M Digitals (P) Ltd.
Proofreader:	Dennis W. Webb
Cover Designer:	Scott Van Atta

Contents

Acknowledgments   **ix**

About the Author   **xi**

Introduction   **xiii**

Part I Engaging the Writer   **1**

1. Catch a Falling Writer by . . .
   Generating Meaningful Discussions   3

2. Catch a Falling Writer by . . .
   Scaffolding Ideas for Writing   5

3. Catch a Falling Writer by . . .
   Using Wordless Picture Books   9

4. Catch a Falling Writer by . . .
   Activating Prior Knowledge   13

5. Catch a Falling Writer by . . .
   Modeling HOW to Write   15

6. Catch a Falling Writer by . . .
   Creating a Vocabulary "Shopping Cart"   17

7. Catch a Falling Writer by . . .
   Motivating With Puppets   20

8. Catch a Falling Writer by . . .
   Encouraging Dramatic Expression   22

9. Catch a Falling Writer by . . .
   Teaching the Purpose of a Web   26

10. Catch a Falling Writer by . . .
    Introducing a Story Frame   29

11. Catch a Falling Writer by . . .
    Maintaining a Motivating Writing Center   32

Part II The Mechanics of Writing   **35**

12. Catch a Falling Writer by . . .
    Correcting the Pencil Grip   37

13. Catch a Falling Writer by . . .
    Using a Variety of Tools   39

14. Catch a Falling Writer by . . .
    Starting With Unlined Paper and Paper Plates   41

15. Catch a Falling Writer by . . .
    Teaching Proper Penmanship Positions   43

16. Catch a Falling Writer by . . .
    Attending to Directionality and Spacing   45

17. Catch a Falling Writer by . . .
    Correcting Errors   47

18. Catch a Falling Writer by . . .
    Articulating Words Aloud   50

19. Catch a Falling Writer by . . .
    Tapping, Stomping, and Jumping Words   52

20. Catch a Falling Writer by . . .
    Practicing Letter Formations and Sight Words   54

21. Catch a Falling Writer by . . .
    Rebuilding Cut-Up Sentences   57

Part III Creating Independence   **61**

22. Catch a Falling Writer by . . .
    Using Verbal Prompts for Self-Editing   63

23. Catch a Falling Writer by . . .
    Offering a Pinch of Praise   66

24. Catch a Falling Writer by . . .
    Recording Oral Responses on Sticky Notes   70

25. Catch a Falling Writer by . . .
    Offering a Variety of Focus Sheets   72

26. Catch a Falling Writer by . . .
    Dealing With Procrastination   75

27. Catch a Falling Writer by . . .
    Using a Variety of "Good" Questions   79

28. Catch a Falling Writer by . . .
    Adding Art, Music, and Drama   82

29. Catch a Falling Writer by . . .
    Connecting Writing With Reading   84

30. Catch a Falling Writer by . . .
    Guiding Writers in Small-Group Instruction   87

Appendix: Focus Sheets   **89**

Recommended Web Sites, Research, and Texts   **97**

Acknowledgments

Corwin gratefully acknowledges the following peer reviewers for their editorial insight and guidance.

Karla Bronzynski
First-Grade Teacher
Eldora-New Providence Schools
President, Iowa Reading Association
Eldora, IA

Renee Nealon
Kindergarten Teacher, NBCT
McDowell Elementary School
Petaluma City School District
Petaluma, CA

Pamela Maslin Sullivan
Assistant Professor
James Madison University
Harrisonburg, VA

About the Author

Connie R. Hebert, EdD, is a nationally acclaimed teacher of teachers, reading specialist, and motivational speaker. Her mission is to help every child become independently literate through the power of teaching. She teaches educators and parents how to "catch" children who are struggling as readers, writers, and thinkers. Connie received a doctorate in educational leadership from Nova Southeastern University, a master of arts in education/ reading from the College of William and Mary, a bachelor of science in education from Framingham State College, and Reading Recovery certification from Lesley University. Experience in the field includes director of reading (K–12), elementary teacher (seven school districts), reading specialist (K–6), gifted and talented teacher, elementary music teacher, and reading recovery teacher (three school districts). She is the author of the books *Catch a Falling Reader, Second Edition* (Corwin, 2007), and *Catch a Falling Teacher* (Corwin, 2006). Other educational materials include four titles published by Crystal Springs Books: *Sight-Word Phrases (PreK–2)* (2002), *Sight-Word Phrases (Grades 1–4)* (2002), *50 Teeny Sight-Word Phrases (PreK–K)* (2008), and *50 Tricky Sight-Word Phrases (Grades 1–3)* (2008). She served nine years as a senior national consultant for SDE (Staff Development for Educators) and three years as a literacy consultant for Macmillan McGraw-Hill's Treasures program. Dr. Hebert is a reading program professor for Nova Southeastern University's Fischler School of Education, teaching teachers around the world through innovative distance learning opportunities. She is a former literacy instructor for Lesley University and has taught language-arts courses for teaching candidates in four Massachusetts state colleges. She has presented literacy training and motivational keynote addresses in 47 states and for many national, state, and European state reading conferences. She can be reached at www.conniehebert.com.

Introduction

As a nation, we have focused a great deal of attention and research on reading instruction. We would be wise to include the power of writing instruction and its reciprocity to reading. *Catch a Falling Writer* is intended to provide educators with strategies for "catching" struggling elementary school writers, including students taking advantage of our special education (SPED) and English language learner (ELL) programs. Classroom teachers, reading specialists, special education teachers, classroom assistants, parents, literacy coaches, and student teachers will benefit from this work.

The topic of writing instruction is extremely relevant today because so many children struggle with basic writing skills that are needed to meet the growing demands of writing in today's schools. Many children currently enter our schools with limited language skills, insufficient coloring and scribbling experiences, weak fine-motor skills, incorrect pencil grip, perfectionist behaviors, and inadequate exposure to letter-sound knowledge. It has become increasingly evident that specific strategies and ideas for teaching "falling writers" is very much needed in a society where a computer mouse and a television remote-control device are more prevalent than pencils and crayons. A *falling writer* is defined as any child who cannot write on or above grade level with independence.

This book is intended to strengthen and anchor the powerful connection between reading and writing. It will shed light on the issue of falling writers before feelings of frustration, defeat, and incompetence take root. Good teachers continually strive to become better teachers by searching for effective tools in the struggle to help children become independent readers, writers, and thinkers. This pursuit requires commitment, patience, flexibility, skill, and sheer will. The foundation for the information provided in this book stems from research-based strategies combined with decades of observation and instruction of children of all ages, training from some of the best teachers and researchers in the world, and years of teaching teachers around the globe.

Falling writers can be identified if we, as teachers and parents, become acutely aware of red flags that often present themselves in the early stages of writing development. The tricky part is that red flags come in a host of different shapes and sizes. These flags often appear during the preschool and kindergarten years but don't always manifest themselves fully until Grade 1.

Some early warning signs among falling writers appear to be more common than others. Teachers and reading specialists who are aware of these behaviors will want to begin where the learner is and build on strengths to move the reader forward. This awareness can lead to a search for contributing factors and, ultimately, a plan of action for each child who appears to be "falling."

Listed below are the most common early warning signs that we should watch for while teaching and guiding young learners. They include, but are not limited to, the following:

(*Note:* Early warning signs do not necessarily appear in this order for any given child.)

- Delayed speech and language skills
- Limited scribbling and drawing skills
- Word retrieval difficulties (trouble "finding" words when retelling, explaining, or describing things, stories, or events)
- Limited prior knowledge, vocabulary, or background experiences
- Directionality issues (right-left, top-bottom, front-back, before-after)
- Limited coloring, drawing, and painting opportunities
- Unusually short attention span when drawing or writing on a whiteboard
- Little or no interest in practicing letter formations
- Little or no attempt at attending to print (doesn't understand that print carries meaning)
- Limited writing vocabulary
- Little or no instant recognition of basic sight words (*yes, no, Mom, a, I*)

- Blinking, yawning, frowning, wiggling, or other unusual behaviors during activities that require coloring or writing
- Pressing down "too hard" when coloring or writing
- Writing words all over the page instead of in a line
- Lips shut tightly when attempting to write unfamiliar words
- Constantly asking, "How do you spell ____?"
- Reading painfully (word-by-word reading with little or no blending of words into phrases)

What can this book do for those who seek to catch a falling writer?

- Offer ideas in a format that is easy to read and understand. This is not a textbook. Ideas and suggestions have been gathered from actual experiences in the field combined with research-based findings.
- Create a conscious awareness of common behaviors in young writers that often become habits.
- Recommend research-based strategies and methods for preventing falling writers from continuing to fall.
- Provide opportunities for educators to confirm, reflect, and enhance their current knowledge of how to teach and assist falling writers on the journey to becoming independent readers, writers, and thinkers.

The best way to read this book is simply to make it a daily practice—reading, reflecting, and perhaps trying one or two strategies each week. You may also want to allow the book to serve as a springboard for teacher book club discussions and debates. *Catch a Falling Writer* is divided into three specific parts: "Engaging the Writer," "The Mechanics of Writing," and "Creating Independence." These three areas were selected as a way of organizing the information into manageable chunks. Segments within each part do not need to be read in any particular order. Teachers of students with special needs as well as those learning a second language will benefit from many of the strategies offered, with modification and differentiation.

It is my sincere hope that this book will inspire each reader to catch every falling student along the universal path to literacy. I firmly believe that when we teach children how to fly as readers and writers, we save them. Reflection on how and why we do what we do, as teachers, is a key to understanding the craft of teaching falling readers and writers. As educators and parents, we often struggle to find the time to actually "think" about our teaching practices and theories. This book was created with that reality in mind. Finally, consider the following as you search for the power between reading and writing:

- We *all* have students who can read well but struggle to write well.
- We have *no* students who can write well but cannot read well.

Now, let's catch our falling writers!

Part I

Engaging the Writer

The purpose of this part of the book is to engage the reader in engaging the writer! A rocket would never get off the ground if its engines failed to engage. The same principle holds true for writers, especially falling writers. Many of these students come to us with some ideas and some skills for writing, but they just cannot seem to engage in the process of writing. Some do not know where to start, while others lack skills and strategies that could move them beyond traditional "I like" stories. Others have ideas, but they are often fragmented, scattered, and disorganized. Still others just cannot think of anything to write. The suggestions in this part offer tools for your teaching toolbox that will engage your students as they write. Ready, set, go!

Author's Note: Although drawing serves as a precursor to writing stories, it is not the author's desire to make it a requirement for all writers. Many falling writers have difficulty drawing, or they simply do not like to draw. Some children just do not like the way they draw, and they do not feel they are good at it. While drawing is always an option before, during, and after writing, it is not a necessity. Many authors will never be illustrators, and many illustrators prefer not to be authors! Encourage students to draw if they would like to, but try not to make it a "have to" with every piece of writing they produce.

In this part, we will focus on the following areas:

Catch a Falling Writer by . . . *Generating Meaningful Discussions*

Catch a Falling Writer by . . . *Scaffolding Ideas for Writing*

Catch a Falling Writer by . . . *Using Wordless Picture Books*

Catch a Falling Writer by . . . *Activating Prior Knowledge*

Catch a Falling Writer by . . . *Modeling HOW to Write*

Catch a Falling Writer by . . . *Creating a Vocabulary "Shopping Cart"*

Catch a Falling Writer by . . . *Motivating With Puppets*

Catch a Falling Writer by . . . *Encouraging Dramatic Expression*

Catch a Falling Writer by . . . *Teaching the Purpose of a Web*

Catch a Falling Writer by . . . *Introducing a Story Frame*

Catch a Falling Writer by . . . *Maintaining a Motivating Writing Center*

1

Catch a Falling Writer by . . .

Generating Meaningful Discussions

The heart of meaningful writing is meaningful chatter.

I f one believes, as I do, that written communication is merely thinking brought down to the pen, then the importance of daily oral communication with children cannot be overemphasized. If we want to produce great writers, we need to produce great thinkers. It's that simple and that hard.

Babies watch us talk and then imitate us. Toddlers copy everything we do and say, and then they begin to ask, "Why?" Preschoolers have so much to say that we sometimes want them to take a break from all the chatter! Primary-grade students learn to wait their turn before speaking, while upper-grade students hope that no one calls on them to speak. Still, I talk to you and you talk to me. But how meaningful is the discussion, and what does this have to do with writing?

What makes it hard? For one thing, we are living in an age where children are no longer "seen and not heard." They have a lot to say, and we would be wise to encourage their thoughts, early attempts at speech and language patterns, and meaningful conversations. Too often, children will ask a question and get a one-word answer, nothing more. One-word responses do indeed answer the question, but they don't extend thinking or toss the "ball" back to the child. For example, a young child might ask, "Is it raining outside today?" The answer might be *yes* or *no*. This is a missed opportunity for generating meaningful conversation that could lead to more words, more ideas, and more language. Let's consider an alternate answer: "I think it might be, but tell me how we could know for sure." This response encourages creative thinking, while also encouraging the child to consider more thoughts on the topic. If the child hesitates to answer, we might say, "I don't hear it on the roof, but that doesn't mean it's not raining. How else could you check?"

Too often, we encounter missed opportunities for engaging in meaningful, thoughtful conversations with children of all ages. The next time a child asks you a question, consider how you might "stretch" their thinking.

2

Catch a Falling Writer by . . .

Scaffolding Ideas for Writing

Ideas are merely twinkling stars in the brain, waiting to be noticed.

"**I**'ve got an idea!" This phrase is probably one of the top ten phrases that kids use when they are feeling creative. In fact, it is often hard to get them to stop offering ideas once they are on a roll! A big issue for falling writers is the line that is drawn in their heads, the one that lies between an idea and the ability to write about it. Have you ever tuned into the "mental dialogue" that goes on within a struggling student who is preparing to write? If not, it is important to take notice, because we must become proficient at "reading our kids." By this, I mean that it is possible to observe mental dialogue if one is tuned into the subtle behaviors and expressions that accompany struggling kids.

Let's examine this further so that what I am suggesting makes sense to those who teach struggling writers and deal with the frustration of coming up with ideas of what to write about. We usually begin with a brainstorming session, generating ideas orally and recording them on a chart or whiteboard. To illustrate, let's say we are discussing a baseball game between two popular teams who played the night before. Students take turns sharing their thoughts, and some seem quite passionate about the game. The teacher might elect to write down some of their ideas on a web about baseball or even list some vocabulary words that are associated with baseball. Some students just listen quietly and don't contribute much. The teacher says, "For journal writing today, we will write about baseball. Does anyone have any questions or want to add about our topic?" Then, off they go to begin their journal-writing assignment.

If we were to zoom in on individuals at this point, we would observe some who are busy gathering their pencils, erasers, and anything else that might help them write. We would see others who have already begun to put ideas onto paper. We might see some students who are copying what the teacher wrote on the chart, so they can use these words and ideas in their own writing. Finally, we would notice some who are simply sitting there, doing nothing. Yes, some may be thinking, and thinking is good and necessary. However, after a while, they are still sitting there and nothing is happening to that journal. These are the children who need help in getting the train out of the station, or it may never leave!

A student who just sits there is quite often the student who has not contributed anything orally to the group's brainstorming session. He or she may have been listening, or not. Either way, the student did not participate for a host of individual reasons. One big reason may be that this child simply cannot relate to this topic. He may have no interest in baseball, or he may have never watched a baseball game. He may be mentally comparing his lack of knowledge to his classmates', and this may be disturbing. It may even block him from wanting to write at all.

Another angle might be that this student is trying to figure out the safest and easiest way to do this assignment and to be done with it! You can almost see this happening if you watch falling writers carefully. They will write something and erase it immediately. They will fidget with their pencil, sharpen it a few times, take things out of their desk, and make themselves appear to be busy. In fact, they will do everything they can to avoid this assignment or to figure out the easiest route. Avoidance behavior is due to a lack of ideas that can be successfully written down on paper with a minimum of errors. Therefore, you might see journal entries like this:

- Baseball is nice. It is fun. I like baseball.
- I played baseball with my friend.
- In baseball, you have to hit the ball and run to the bases.
- My brother plays baseball. His team wins a lot. I go to the games, too.

Students who write like this have basically found a way to write about the assigned topic by sticking with safe, easy-to-spell sight words and simple phrases. If you ask them to write more, they will simply add more short phrases with little creativity or thought. They are more interested in getting it done than in getting it right.

Scaffolding ideas is an art, and teachers who know how to do it can help falling writers enormously. The best way to help children who are "stuck" on an idea is to have an oral conversation with them before they write, individually. Here is how one scenario might go:

(*Note:* Student's responses are in bold print.)

"How's it going, Jonathan?"

"Good."

"Tell me a little about baseball before you start writing in your journal."

"It's fun."

"Let me ask you this, Jonathan. If a kid from another country came to the United States and never heard of baseball before, what would you tell her about it?"

"It's where you hit a ball and run the bases."

"What else would you tell her so that she really understands how we play it?"

"Well, you have to go to all three bases and then to home base in order to score a point."

"Does everyone get to go to home base just for hitting a ball?"

"No! You can get people out by touching them with the ball."

"So what do we call that?"

"An out!"

"Can you tell me that in a whole sentence, Jonathan? Start with 'When someone hits the ball . . .'"

"When someone hits the ball, they run to the bases and try not to get out."

"Excellent! Now, tell me again; what are three things that someone would need to know about baseball if they knew *nothing* about it?"

Whatever Jonathan says, at this point, is what you will encourage him to write in his journal. This meaningful conversation served as a springboard for the topic because it took the student away from focusing on the "act of writing" into the "act of thinking" by scaffolding ideas. Remember that writing is just thinking brought down to the pen. By engaging in meaningful discussions while using prompts that scaffold one's thinking, we can help falling writers move forward in productive, creative ways. The art of scaffolding is not easy; it takes practice. It is, however, essential to the process of helping struggling writers write better!

3

Catch a Falling Writer by . . .

Using Wordless Picture Books

If a picture can get a child to talk, why not use it?

Wordless picture books can reveal a great deal of information about a child's oral language development. We can hear how they use words to convey meaning when describing something. We can observe how they retrieve words and connect them into phrases or sentences. We can note their diction, phrasing, and intonation. Much can be learned from asking a child to "read" the pictures in a wordless book.

Wordless picture books can easily be divided into three main levels. Book levels are based on a combination of picture complexity, implications for meaning, sequence of events, objects and actions on each page, story line, picture support, and oral language requirements for clear understanding. A description of each level follows:

LEVEL A: "SMALL TALK" BOOKS

This level includes books with the following characteristics:

- One or two pictures on each page
- Limited story plots (if any)
- Interaction involves mainly "point and say"
- Familiar objects, animals, colors, and shapes
- Large pictures, sometimes using both left and right pages for one scene
- Details within pictures tend to be large and simple
- Book titles and cover pictures are simple and to the point
- Limited inference and prediction needed to gain meaning
- Early concepts about print can be reinforced easily

LEVEL B: "MORE TALK" BOOKS

This level includes books with the following characteristics:

- Fairly detailed pictures on *each* page
- Greater opportunities to predict plots in sequential order
- Several objects or scenes on each page
- Include concepts such as shapes, colors, school, curiosity, mischief, eating out, and so forth
- Story titles require more inference about the main idea
- Detailed cover pictures, requiring greater prediction and more complex vocabulary
- Picture layout includes pictures on left and right pages with *new* events or objects on each
- Requires that students make predictions, draw conclusions, search for details within scenes, analyze cause-and-effect relationships, and interact more with the book in order to draw meaning

LEVEL C: "BIG TALK" BOOKS

This level includes books with the following characteristics:

- Requires greater attention to details and event sequences, requires complex predictions, and includes more vocabulary that is descriptive.

- Pictures are filled with details and clues that call upon critical-thinking and problem-solving skills
- Pictures include artistic details that reveal facial expressions and body language; they are more complicated and detailed than easier levels
- Multi-snapshot scenes that resemble hand-drawn filmstrips offer opportunities for reinforcing directional movements, return sweep, voice-print match, and sequencing of events
- Offer more opportunities for fluent oral phrasing, vocal expression, oral sentence structure, and diction
- Serve as writing prompts for stories that can be written to accompany these books

Below are suggestions for reading wordless picture books together:

- ➤ Discuss the title and cover picture. Ask, "What is this story about? How do you know? What do you notice in the cover picture? Tell me more!"
- ➤ Begin "reading" the story by modeling complete oral sentences. For example, "One day, a bird was sitting on a tree and saw a big red apple fall off a branch."
- ➤ Let the child tell the story, using the pictures for support and meaning. Encourage her to speak in complete sentences. Take turns doing this if it is difficult for the child. Encourage descriptive talk; ask questions such as "What color is it?" "Where is it?" "What else can we say about this dog?" "Is the dog happy, sad, small, or big?"
- ➤ Ask the child open-ended "prediction" questions between pages: "What do you think might happen next?" "What makes you think so?" "Can you guess what they might do on the next page?" "Do you think they are happy?" "How do you know?"
- ➤ Ask the child to reread the whole story, this time without questions or interruptions.
- ➤ Encourage the child to dictate a sentence to you about the story or to write a sentence to go with a picture in the story. You can write the dictated sentence on paper, and then ask the child to draw a picture to go with it.

By reading wordless picture books, a child's literacy development will benefit in many ways. By using wordless picture books as an assessment to learn more about the way in which children use oral language to convey meaning, we are able to learn a great deal about what the child brings to early literacy development. Wordless books not only serve as great oral language tools, but they also provide wonderful writing prompts for students who often say, "I can't think of anything to write!"

Remember, a picture speaks a thousand words.

4

Catch a Falling Writer by . . .

Activating Prior Knowledge

Prior knowledge acts as a key to many doorways of understanding.

H ere is an important question for us to ponder: Is prior knowledge the main determinant of comprehension? Yes or no? The answer is "Yes!" It is the key to a treasure chest of greater comprehension if it is stocked properly and maintained regularly. If you don't believe me, try reading a passage from a journal about a subject that you know *nothing* about. Watch what happens to comprehension, fluency, motivation, and recall. Now, try writing about that same subject! Without prior knowledge, we are lost in an unknown sea, searching for a way to reach a familiar shore. In other words, everything we experience in life goes into a treasure chest of prior knowledge that is stored in the brain. When the chest is filled with concepts, words, ideas, and a variety of sensory experiences, we are better able to tap into a rich storehouse when we attempt to read and write. Conversely, when the chest is filled with experiences that are limited to daily routines, television, and video games (with limited exposure to print and little oral communication), we are unable to efficiently and adequately bring meaning to the act of literacy.

It is critically important, as teachers of readers and writers, that we continuously stock the treasure chest of prior knowledge for children, especially those who are in danger of "falling." Children cannot be expected to write sentences and stories that are rich in meaning, vocabulary usage, and descriptive language if their storehouse of prior knowledge is disabled or dysfunctional. Here are suggestions for building and activating prior knowledge in learners who struggle:

> ➢ Read aloud *daily*, and engage falling writers in meaningful discussions that will give their brains plenty of practice with recalling details, defining concepts and vocabulary, using new words in complete sentences, describing what the author meant, making comparisons, and generating lots of predictions.
> ➢ Give students *daily* opportunities to listen to audiobooks to increase exposure to concepts, oral language structures, fluent phrasing, new vocabulary, sequences of events, visual tracking skills, and the role of punctuation.
> ➢ Offer students a variety of ways to respond to text to activate prior knowledge (webs, graphic organizers, art, role-playing, puppetry, paired discussions, journal entries, etc.).
> ➢ Expose falling writers to many different reference materials, such as dictionaries with both definitions and pictures, thesauruses that offer multiple alternatives to everyday words, informational text that expands a child's view of the world, and magazines that enlighten and inform.
> ➢ Suggest that students draw pictures or find photos and pictures from magazines to act as a diving board for writing. If a picture speaks a thousand words, why not use one to activate prior knowledge and get the thinking going?
> ➢ Provide daily opportunities for falling writers to *read, read, read*. They should be encouraged to read anything and everything they can get their hands on! The more they read, the greater their treasure chest of prior knowledge will be.

When we focus on building a storehouse of prior knowledge and then engage students in daily actions that help their brains to activate this knowledge, we are moving them forward in new and productive ways. In essence, we are giving them the tools they need to independently use their very own treasure chest of prior knowledge. Ahoy, mates!

5

Catch a Falling
Writer by . . .

Modeling HOW to Write

Show me how, and I will know how.

Modeling is one of most powerful teaching tools available, and it's free! All we have to do is be willing to show kids "how," and then guide them as they try their best to copy our efforts. Think about this for a moment. If you want to learn how to ski, you watch competent skiers, ski. If you want to learn how to cook, you watch gifted cooks, cook. If you want to learn how to speak in public, you watch effective speakers. Then, with knowledge, skill, practice, and perseverance, you can learn anything! Children need to know how to write so that they have a solid concept of what good writing is and what good writers do. Without an initial understanding of what is expected, they tend to wander around a maze of twists and turns in their early school years. Time, practice, and necessity will eventually force them to adhere to the standards expected of them in the upper grades, but why not show them the way at an early age? Modeling is the key, and we would be wise to use it to its full extent.

Consider several suggestions for showing children how to write:

> ➢ Use the Shared Writing approach to model the act of writing, spacing, voice-print match, directionality, sentence

structure, conventional sight-word spellings, punctuation, letter-sound sequences, creativity, and the writing process.

➢ Use the Interactive Writing approach to guide children *as* they write by providing interactive feedback, corrections, help, support, reminders, suggestions, spelling strategies, and letter formation instruction.

➢ Allow students to draw, before or after they write. This will serve to bring meaning to their written creations and to support their ideas through the act of drawing.

➢ Use the Writer's Workshop approach to model brainstorming strategies, inventive spelling, descriptive language, revision and editing processes, use of the dictionary and thesaurus, and Author's Chair (an approach where students read their writing aloud, while sitting in a "special" chair).

➢ Use the whiteboard to teach proper letter formation, proper pencil grip, legibility, automaticity, sight words, correct upper- and lowercase usage, and appropriate handwriting posture.

➢ Use the chalkboard to have children write, erase, and write it again in the dust; trace over dotted letters several times; practice with their pointer finger to form numbers and letters; use a wet paintbrush to practice formations (without allowing water to drip from the brush); and use the side of chalk to make big, bubble letters with correct formations.

➢ Use dark construction paper to teach children how to form letters with paintbrushes of different sizes and how to write letters quickly and fluently.

➢ Use fine-line markers to model the amount of pressure needed to form letters accurately and quickly.

➢ Use simple, direct verbal commands, such as "Down, up, and around" or "Down, trace back up, around, down," to model how letters are formed. Have children verbally copy your commands *as* they form letters on their own.

➢ Use large poster board to allow children with fine-motor-skill issues to make *big* shapes, to trace *big* letters and numbers, to practice over and over on top of dotted letters, and to apply appropriate pressure using big, fat markers and paintbrushes.

Here is the bottom line: model, model, and model. Then, model some more!

6

Catch a Falling
Writer by . . .

*Creating a Vocabulary
"Shopping Cart"*

When the vocabulary gets tough, the tough go shopping!

Vocabulary is as important to reading and writing as bread and water are to life. I know you will agree that many children simply do not have a well-stocked storehouse of words to draw upon as they decode and comprehend new texts. Falling readers and writers rely mainly on two things to support their efforts: memory and letter sounds. They resort to writing only words that they can "see" in their head or can sound out easily and clearly. If the word does not fall into one of these two categories, the child will most likely select another word that is easier or simply give up. These options are limiting, frustrating, and ineffective as students move along from grade to grade.

What do we do to give children more options in the area of vocabulary development? The answer is simple but hard to do without daily commitment and effort. We must create a "shopping cart" of words that students can build, use, and expand. As they gain momentum in the area of written language, they will be able to draw on this shopping cart to "purchase" new and different vocabulary selections. They must, however, create the shopping cart, and this requires that they be exposed to an abundance of words on a daily basis.

Here are the steps for creating a vocabulary shopping cart for falling writers in all grade levels:

1. The student must listen to an audiobook daily with the goal of identifying at least five words in each book.

2. The student must take these five words and find out what they mean. This can be accomplished by consulting with peers, other adults, a dictionary, or a thesaurus.

3. By the end of the day, the child writes or types the five vocabulary words into a personal "shopping cart."

4. The next morning, the child needs to read the five new shopping cart words to someone and briefly describe what each word means or use it in a sentence.

5. The child listens to a new audiobook that day and selects five new words from that book. Steps 2 through 5 are then repeated for 30 consecutive days.

6. On Day 30, the student will have acquired 150 vocabulary words as an initial shopping cart "inventory."

7. It is recommended that the student be encouraged to use these words throughout the 30-day cycle when journaling, for morning messages, at home, for seatwork assignments, as weekly spelling words, and during whiteboard practice.

8. The teacher may want to give the child 30 days to use the 150 words before starting a new 30-day cycle to generate more "inventory" for the shopping cart.

9. Students should be encouraged to work with their words by alphabetizing them, writing them in sentences, illustrating them, counting syllables within words, scrambling letters, identifying vowels and consonants, or simply reading them daily.

10. Students might also want to swap words in their cart with words from other vocabulary shopping carts. They can even "price" their words and play store with others in an effort to build their inventory!

The ideas for a vocabulary shopping cart are endless. Once you get kids started on this, they will learn to rely on their cart as a tool and a daily activity. The key to success with this, however, is the need for a *daily* commitment on the part of the student and teacher. One also needs to build a good repertoire of audiobooks and advocate for a working listening center, but you can do it! Remember, the squeaky wheel gets the oil!

7

Catch a Falling
Writer by . . .

Motivating With Puppets

Puppets are really truly amazing teachers.

As I was walking through a neighborhood on Halloween with my son, I overheard a group of kids whispering and pointing toward us. As we approached, they stopped and told me that they knew me. They couldn't quite place who I was or how they knew me, but they kept saying they knew me. After a few seconds, one of them pointed right at me and said, "Oh yeah, you're the lady with Max, the mouse. You came into our first grade!" This group of students was now in sixth grade, and although they forgot my name, they remembered me through my mouse puppet, Max! Amazing . . .

I can tell you hundreds of similar stories from kids in all the many schools and districts I taught in. I have always believed in the "power" of puppets because they capture a child's attention faster than anything I have ever seen. Puppets motivate children to attend to a task at hand because they are fun, cute, fascinating to watch, and childlike. Perhaps a puppet's greatest power lies in its ability to hold attention for long periods of time, depending on the skill of the puppeteer.

If you shy away from using puppets because they feel awkward to handle or difficult to "make talk," just get a simple hand puppet and have the puppet talk into your ear. There's no need for the puppet to talk at all. I did this with Max because so many teachers told me they don't use puppets because they "don't do voices well." This is a legitimate concern, but you can simply have the puppet turn to "whisper" into your ear, and then you respond to that. For example, I ask Max to tell us what good writers do when they first think of an idea, and then I hold him to my ear and wiggle him a bit. I then hold him back and look at him while exclaiming, "Oh, Max! You are *so* smart. Yes, good writers do brainstorm ideas, but what exactly does *brainstorm* mean, Max?" We go back and forth like this, and I even throw in silly comments that Max "makes" about cheese in the classroom! The kids are hysterical, and it doesn't matter to them if Max is actually talking or if he isn't. I am manipulating the conversation, but Max is the star. They listen to Max, no matter what!

Here are a few topics of conversation around writing that you might initiate with the puppet so that struggling students tune into a problem or issue more attentively than they normally would without the use of a puppet:

- ➤ Right and wrong pencil grip
- ➤ Thinking of a title for a story
- ➤ Using describing words, or adjectives, in our writing
- ➤ Leaving out the punctuation
- ➤ Checking for correct upper- and lowercase letter formations
- ➤ Complete sentences versus phrases
- ➤ Adding more to a story when we are stuck
- ➤ Checking to see if it makes sense and looks right
- ➤ Using a dictionary or thesaurus
- ➤ Rereading is a good idea
- ➤ Adding more to a story
- ➤ Using a web to focus ideas
- ➤ Writing a story to go with a wordless book

If you hesitate to use puppets because you are shy, afraid, tired, or unsure, I have one response for you: Do it anyway!! The rewards are *so* worth it. Don't underestimate the power of a sock with two buttons sewn on it for eyes. It's really a teacher in disguise!

8

Catch a Falling Writer by . . .

Encouraging Dramatic Expression

Imagination is a launch pad for creative writing.

If we truly want to develop creative thinking among our falling writers, we must learn how to launch the imagination. All of us have an imagination, but kids seem to come with an extra dose of it! They are mentally free to dream all sorts of dreams and create all sorts of things, if given the opportunity. Our work with falling writers offers daily chances to awaken the imagination and stimulate fresh ideas for writing.

I am reminded of a workshop I attended, years ago, in Virginia. I was a young, enthusiastic teacher who wanted to learn and grow. I was given the opportunity to do so by a teacher who taught us how to awaken creative expression in kids while also improving their writing skills. I remember trying all sorts of wonderful exercises and having great fun with my colleagues that day. Although I can't remember the face or name of the teacher who enlightened me about the power of dramatic expression, I can pass along things I did that really helped my students.

Here are a few dramatic activities to try with kids of all ages:

> *Giant Strawberry:* Have the children stand up and tell them to imagine that a very red strawberry is in front of them on the floor. Begin your dialogue by saying, "Oh my! Look! It's growing and growing and growing. It is as high as the ceiling and as round as you can imagine. What's this? You see a small door on the side of your strawberry. Well, pull the handle. Pull it harder. It's open! What are we waiting for? Pull off your shoes, and let's climb inside! OK, we're inside the strawberry. Take out your flashlight that's in your pocket, of course. *Wow!* Who can describe what this feels like on your feet? Jump up and down. Let's sit down. How does this feel? Hey, look up! What do you see? Tell me more. OK, let's feel the sidewall with both hands. Yuck! Who can describe that feeling? What does it smell like? Hey, I've got a great idea! Let's take a big bite out of the side of the strawberry. How does yours taste? Uh, oh—the strawberry is shrinking. Hurry and get out! Shut the door behind you. You made it!" Now, have them draw a picture of their very own giant fruit and then write some words next to it that describe it.

> *Convince Me:* Sit across from a friend and decide who will be Partner A and who will be Partner B. "Now listen carefully, so you'll know what to do. In between the two of you, there is a giant cookie! It is *the* biggest, most delicious cookie either of you has ever, ever seen, and you are very hungry. In fact, you haven't eaten a thing all day, so you really and truly want to eat this cookie. Partner A, when I say *go*, you will have one minute to convince your partner why *you* should be the one to eat this cookie. Partner B will listen to you without saying one word! When I say *stop*, please stop. After one minute, we will switch roles, and Partner B, you will have one minute to convince Partner A why you need to eat that cookie! Remember to use your words and good ideas to convince your partner. Remember also to be a good listener while your partner is speaking."

> **Repeat *Convince Me:*** Use the following scenarios (or come up with a few of your own!). The idea is to get kids talking,

imagining, and using language in a variety of expressive ways.

- o Pretend Partner A is a teenager and Partner B is the parent. "Teenagers, you just got your license today. You have one minute to convince your parent why you need the car tonight. Parents will then have one minute to convince their teenager why they need the car tonight."
- o Pretend Partner A is the teacher and Partner B is the student. "Teachers, you have one minute to teach your partner how to make a lunch to bring to school. Students, you will have one minute to tell your teacher all the reasons why you can't possibly make your lunch to bring to school."
- o Pretend that you have a lunch box sitting between you and your partner. "Inside the lunch box is a porcupine. She is stuck! You have one minute to convince your partner that you know how to get that porcupine out of the lunch box. Then we'll switch and see how your partner would get her out!"
- o Pretend that your partner is stuck in the top of a palm tree and can't come down. A hurricane is coming, and the winds are getting stronger and stronger. "You have one minute to tell your partner how you will help him get down before the hurricane hits. Then we will switch, and your partner will have one minute to tell you why he will *not* come down, no matter what you say or do!"

➤ *May I help you?* In this small-group dramatic activity, three children are seated at a table pretending to look over a menu. Another child plays the role of a server on the first day of work. This person has *never* been a server before. The three children must act like the *pickiest* eaters in the world, describing exactly how they want and don't want their food. For example, when ordering drinks, one might say to the server, "I will have a large diet cola with exactly four ice cubes, no straw, and no bubbles please!" Another might say, "I will have ice tea with a slice of lemon that has no peel on it, a piece of lime on the side with lots of sugar, and no ice cubes please." The server has to repeat the orders and can't write them down. After the server "delivers" the drinks, the customers can make one comment to the server about their drink. Then, switch places and let the server be a customer and a customer be the brand new server!

As you might imagine, dramatic activities, like those listed above, build creative expression, oral language skills, vocabulary usage, and critical thinking. In addition, each activity can serve as a "launch pad" for creative writing. If you allow students to participate in dramatic activities on a frequent basis, you will find that their ability to think of ideas to write improves. You may also cultivate a bunch of future actors who have a flair for creative expression. To be or not to be? you might ask. Yes, dramatic play *should* be a part of your language-arts block, daily—especially for falling writers.

9

Catch a Falling Writer by . . .

Teaching the Purpose of a Web

If a web can help a spider, think of what it can do for a writer.

If a spider was a writer, I am certain it would use a web to organize its thoughts, steps, and goals. Actually, a spider is a good example of how we should guide students in setting up their writing so that they stay on task and focus on the end result. Too often, we see fragmentation in our students' writing. By this I mean that students will start writing about a topic and then get sidetracked. They add things that are unrelated to the topic or, in some cases, incomplete. Some kids actually stop writing when they don't have a plan or a map to keep them focused.

The problem with webs is that too many kids rely on the teacher to provide one for them. They only use them when the teacher says they have to! The other problem lies in the heart of a web. Students just don't know *why* they need to complete a web before they write. Many kids, especially falling writers, think it's just one more big assignment to complete, and by the time they are done with it, they don't want to write any more! So it's counterproductive.

I am a strong advocate for giving students a purpose for everything we teach them, especially when it is a tool that will help them for years to come. If they don't know *why* they should do something, then why do it? Falling writers want to escape from writing because it is time-consuming, tedious, and stressful for them. If they do not "buy into" the reasons for taking time to do a web, they will not use one as a strategy for generating ideas and planning a course of action. It is our responsibility to teach students not only *how* to do a web, but *why* they should do one.

Here are some of the reasons for generating a web prior to writing (please add your own as well):

- A web can save time because it helps us to gather our thoughts in one place, as a spider does with bugs!
- Our brains need to think before we write, and a web gives us that chance.
- When we put a topic in the center of a web, we can focus on just that topic. Otherwise, we sometimes write about all different topics.
- Once we have a reason for writing, we can branch out and generate ideas to support our topic. The "arms" of a web are a place for us to record our ideas. Good writers brainstorm ideas before they write.
- A web can serve as a map if you use it for that purpose. For example, if you were going to write a report about your state, you would put the name of your state in the center of the web. Then you would draw five lines or arms that would branch out from the center. On these arms you would write five different things that you want to know about your state. They might be population, climate, industries, capital, and tourist attractions. From these five main areas, you might map out three things from each one that you will explore. (If you include more than three, you probably won't complete all five areas, so stick with three.) For instance, under population, you might want to look into the different cultures that live in your state, animal populations, and changes in your state's population in the last five years. This is a great map and a wonderful start!
- With young falling writers, you can use drawings or magazine pictures with words written under them to illustrate the uses of a web. For example, if the students were learning

about good nutrition, you, the teacher, would paste a picture of healthy foods in the center of a chart. Then, you would draw five arms from the center and have the kids name the five food groups. You can cut out and paste a picture of each food group under the name. Then, the kids can find pictures of foods that go with each food group category and write the names under each picture. Preschoolers can dictate the names, and the teacher can write them under their pictures. The main idea here is to teach young children how a web can serve as a framework for writing about a topic.

- Falling writers would do well with a blank web that can serve as a template for their writing. I suggest giving them a folder of blank webs to keep with their writing journals. Before they write, they will use the web to frame their thoughts and brainstorm ideas about whatever topic they want to write about.

- Never assume that kids know *why* they are doing something, even after you think you have explained it to them! Every now and then, ask a falling writer why a web is important and how it can help. Many kids forget why they do things because it just becomes routine. Keeping them "on their toes" is a key to cementing the purpose of using a web.

Add your own reasons for doing webs:

_____

_____

_____

A web is a wonderful tool for writers, if they know why they need one. When you take the time to teach them how it can help them, they will come to see how it will make them a better writer. Be careful not to insist that children create a web for every writing task they do. It will lose its power! We want kids to use tools and strategies when appropriate and useful. Be sure to give them examples of when you, yourself, might use a web and when you would not.

Experience teaches us that writing will come more easily for falling writers if we give them a variety of tools for their writer's toolbox. Teach them *why* they need a web, and see what happens!

10

Catch a Falling
Writer by . . .

Introducing a Story Frame

Stories are like houses. They need good sturdy frames.

Construction workers know that their plans to build a house must include a frame that will support all other necessary features. Without the frame, how would you add a door, window, or roof? This same process applies to creative story writing. Teach your falling writers this analogy, and they will understand the purpose of a story frame. Then, teach them what a frame might look like. Included is an example of a basic frame that can be written on a chart or reproduced as a handout for students to refer to.

This story takes place _____.

_____ is a character in the story, and he/she likes

to _____ but doesn't like to _____.

The problem is that_____

and then _____. After that, _____.

The problem is solved when _____.

Following the basic frame example, select a familiar story such as *Goldilocks and the Three Bears.* Invite the children to help you fill in the story frame with what they already know about the story. While they are brainstorming, record responses on the lines, and "share the pen" with those who can assist you with this process. When complete, it might look something like this:

This story takes place in a house in the woods. Goldilocks is a character in the story, and she likes to taste soup, sit in chairs, and try out beds but doesn't like to get caught by three bears! The problem is that Goldilocks goes into a house and then finds out that it belongs to three bears. After that, Goldilocks runs home and tells her mom what she's done. The problem is solved when she goes back to the three bears' house and says she is sorry. She never goes into a stranger's house again.

You and the students will want to read it aloud together, as a shared reading. Then encourage students to change the story by having a different problem and a different solution. Once again, students will brainstorm while you record responses. When complete, the frame might look something like this:

This story takes place in the school library at night. Goldilocks is a character in the story, and she likes to read but doesn't like to go to the library during the day. The problem is that Goldilocks sneaks into the library at night and then pulls out several books. Three shelves fall over, and the library is a big mess! After that, she has to spend the whole night picking up and stacking all the books. The problem is solved when Goldilocks decides she'd better go to the library during the day with her class.

You may decide to repeat this process with several more familiar stories during the course of several weeks, especially with falling writers. Once they understand the use and benefits of this simple format, you will want to teach them what the different components of a story frame are. This will assist them in "owning" the story frame as a tool for their own writing. Here are the main components of a basic frame:

- Setting
- Main character
- Character likes and dislikes
- Problem
- Consequence
- Solution

Note: You may want to add or revise these components based on the grade level of your students.

Teaching students to use a story frame provides another tool that will assist them with adding key components to a story, sequencing ideas within the story, and building critical-thinking skills to enrich their creative writing. A sturdy story needs a sturdy frame!

11

Catch a Falling
Writer by . . .

Maintaining a Motivating Writing Center

*If classroom writing centers were set up like kitchens are,
kids would cook up some delicious stories!*

If classroom writing centers were set up like kitchens are, kids
would cook up some delicious stories!

I firmly believe that every elementary classroom in every
elementary school should have a well-stocked and carefully
organized writing center in it! All it takes is a little time and
effort to set up an inviting center where students will want to
visit often. When a classroom writing center is unavailable,
many students write only when assigned to do so. This leaves
little, if any, opportunity for adequate development of written
expression. It also limits students to very few choices.
Remember that writing is just thinking brought down to the
pen. If we want to get the pen moving in a variety of creative

ways, we must get the "thinking" flowing in new and exciting ways.

Below is a suggested list of items you will want to consider when setting up a writing center in your classroom:

- ➢ A variety of pens, pencils, and fine-line markers
- ➢ Different kinds of dictionaries
- ➢ An accordion file full of pictures from magazines, calendars, catalogs, and so forth, filed by subject category for easy access
- ➢ A basket filled with wordless books
- ➢ A basket filled with sight-word phrases
- ➢ Laminated strips with suggested titles written on them
- ➢ Laminated strips with open-ended sentences written on them
- ➢ White correction tape
- ➢ Bins or folders for unfinished and finished work
- ➢ A variety of stickers for use when students prefer not to draw
- ➢ A selection of different types of assembled blank books (paper-plate books, lunch-bag books, construction-paper booklets, composition books, teeny-size books, etc.)
- ➢ A thesaurus
- ➢ Alphabet charts (PreK–Grade 2)
- ➢ Paper of different sizes and different types
- ➢ Rulers and transparent-tape dispensers
- ➢ A variety of magazines

After setting up your center, you will want to give your students a "tour" and encourage them to brainstorm all different ways of using these materials for written communication. Here are some activities you might want to add to the class list:

- ➢ Choose five sight-word phrases and use them in five written sentences.
- ➢ Write a story to go with a wordless book.
- ➢ Choose a title strip, and write a poem to go with it.
- ➢ Select three pictures out of the picture file, and use each of them in a story.
- ➢ Choose an open-ended strip and finish it (e.g., If I were invisible I would . . .).
- ➢ Find five words in the dictionary that you never knew. Write each word and its definition in a paper-plate book.

➢ Use stickers to create a lunch-bag story. Be sure to write a story to go with the stickers you choose.

➢ Choose a wordless book, and write a "backward" story. Start with the last page of the book and work toward the front! Then read your story to someone while he looks at the pictures from back to front.

➢ Look through some magazines, and find five pictures that tell a story. Tape them into a blank book, and write the story to go with them.

➢ Interview a friend in your class. Find out at least eight things about them. Be sure to write your questions down and their answers, too.

➢ Write a letter to your favorite author. Tell them why they are your favorite, and ask them three questions.

➢ Write down five words. Look them up in the thesaurus, and write down the words that mean the same thing. Draw a picture to go with each set of words.

➢ Practice writing all the letters of the alphabet with a fine-line marker. See if you can write them without pressing down too hard and without hearing the marker as you write. Press lightly and form your letters quickly.

The list is endless, but you get the point here. Build them a place to write, and they will come and write! After they write, they can publish their special books. You may want to go a step further and check out various Web sites on the Internet for companies that publish books for children. Kids love seeing their work in published formats!

Part II

The Mechanics of Writing

Writers need tools just like plumbers, painters, mechanics, and builders do. Writers need to know what to do with these tools, and they need to be corrected when they are not using them properly. In other words, we must teach falling writers the mechanics of writing if we are going to keep them from falling further. You might ask what is meant by the term *mechanics of writing*. Well, the tendency is to think of writing as a creative, personal, and engaging act—and it is! However, the developmental process necessary to become an independent writer requires us to know the basics. Too often, we see children who give up in the middle of writing something because their hand hurts. We see others who just do not know where to start or some who have forgotten how to form a letter, so they stop. We must teach the mechanics of writing, so that it *can* be creative, personal, and engaging.

In this part, we will focus on specific strategies for addressing the following areas:

Catch a Falling Writer by . . . *Correcting the Pencil Grip*

Catch a Falling Writer by . . . *Using a Variety of Tools*

Catch a Falling Writer by . . . *Starting With Unlined Paper and Paper Plates*

Catch a Falling Writer by . . . *Teaching Proper Penmanship Positions*

Catch a Falling Writer by . . . *Attending to Directionality and Spacing*

Catch a Falling Writer by . . . *Correcting Errors*

Catch a Falling Writer by . . . *Articulating Words Aloud*

Catch a Falling Writer by . . . *Tapping, Stomping, and Jumping Words*

Catch a Falling Writer by . . . *Practicing Letter Formations and Sight Words*

Catch a Falling Writer by . . . *Rebuilding Cut-Up Sentences*

12

Catch a Falling
Writer by . . .

Correcting the Pencil Grip

If I hold a hammer the wrong way, I may not hit the nail on the head.

Many falling writers hold their pencils, crayons, and markers incorrectly. This problem begins during the preschool years, and it is very difficult to correct when it becomes habitual. The main issue with using an incorrect pencil grip is the strain it causes in the fingers and within the muscles of the hand. We want to watch how children hold their writing tools and fix improper positions immediately, so they will write with ease.

Consider the following points:

IMPORTANT TO KNOW

1. The proper way to hold a writing tool is to place it between the third finger and thumb. Then, bring the second finger (pointer) down on top and squeeze, completing the hold.

2. Many falling writers hold their pencils and crayons with three fingers wrapped around it and the thumb underneath. This adds some strain to the muscles in the fingers and hand and causes the writer to have trouble forming letters and numbers easily.

3. Notice whether a writer is "hooking" the hand because of an improper pencil grip. Hooking the hand will put pressure on the wrist and sometimes prevent the child from seeing the letters because the hand is covering them up.

SOLUTIONS

1. One of the best ways I have found to fix an improper pencil grip is to teach the writer to press a fat cotton ball between the third finger and the pencil. Once the cotton ball is in place, the thumb and pointer finger come together to "pinch" the pencil, thus producing the proper hold. Every time the student goes back to the former way of holding the pencil, the cotton ball will fall. Their job is to pick the cotton ball up, every single time, and put it back between the third finger and the pencil. Eventually, they will learn to keep pressing that finger against the cotton ball until they don't need the ball any longer!

2. Another way to help writers is to put an adhesive bandage on their third finger, and teach them to press the pencil against the soft part of the adhesive bandage while squeezing the pencil with the thumb and pointer finger. Students can draw a face on their writer's bandage or use colorful adhesive bandages to make it fun and different. Adhesive bandages are not as effective as cotton balls because writers can go back to their former grip without any consequences. But for some students, squeezing the pencil against the bandage is just right. Both the cotton ball and the bandage seem to be more effective than a fat rubber grip because they bring attention directly to that important third finger.

THINKING IT OVER

How often do you actually watch students write so that you notice how they are holding their writing tools?

13

Catch a Falling Writer by . . .

Using a Variety of Tools

Why do we all have a favorite pen?

Too often, we can find only one tool for students to write with in school. It is usually a #2 pencil! If you study a pencil, however, you will notice that it is thin and long. It may be fine for some children to hold onto, but not for others. Falling writers do better when we offer them a variety of tools to write with. If they never get to experiment with different types, they will not know what works best for them.

Consider the following points:

IMPORTANT TO KNOW

1. Pencils may not be the best tools for writing for two reasons: (a) there isn't much to hold onto, and (b) the lead is visually light in color on the paper.

2. Falling writers tend to press down too hard when they write. Either they are trying so hard to make it perfectly, or they can't remember which way the letter goes. Thus, they press down and form their letters slowly and deliberately. Encourage students to press down lightly with their marker or roller-ball pen. These tools help letters to "flow" as opposed to other writing tools.

3. It is worth taking a trip to an office supply store to see all the different types of writing tools available on the market.

SOLUTIONS

1. A set of fine-line markers and mechanical pencils seem to work best for most falling writers. The print is visually bolder when writing with a fine-line marker, and the plastic casing seems to be easier to grip than the wood of a pencil. Writing with a marker is also better for forming letters smoothly and easily. Mechanical pencils, for math coursework, tend to last longer than wooden pencils, and they come in different lead thicknesses. A #7 or #9 lead size is best for students who struggle because they tend to press down hard when they write. These sizes are stronger and tend to break less easily.

2. Fat markers and fat crayons fit more easily in the hands of some falling writers. Roller-ball pens help the letter "glide" onto the page, and they may be just right for some kids.

THINKING IT OVER

Do you have a variety of writing tools in your classroom or home for children to experiment with? If children feel successful using one type over another, are they allowed to use it, or are they expected to conform to using the same tool as their peers?

14

Catch a Falling
Writer by . . .

Starting With Unlined Paper and Paper Plates

Lines in the road are necessary but restrictive.

Young writers often focus on whether their letters need to touch the top line, middle line, or bottom line on their lined, grade-level paper. This takes the focus away from proper formation and automaticity and brings it to the lines on the paper. Remove the lines, and then we can teach falling writers how to form their letters automatically and easily.

Consider the following points:

IMPORTANT TO KNOW

1. Falling writers find it difficult to focus on too many things at once. It is better to allow them to cement the proper formation of letters and to write with ease than to expect letters that fit perfectly within prescribed lines.

2. Many writers need opportunities to trace over *big* shapes, letters, and numbers on *big* poster board. This helps their

hand and arm muscles to grow strong while also allowing them to see what they are writing in a *big* way.

3. If we use the same paper for all students, we may find that some of them "turn off" to writing, because they just cannot remember which line their letters need to touch. Take the focus away from fitting letters within lines and move it to forming letters properly. Once this is firmly established, falling writers can shift to their lined grade-level paper.

SOLUTIONS

1. Encourage falling writers to use books that you (or they) have assembled out of unlined oak tag, construction paper, poster board, or paper plates. Even though we teach all students how to write letters and numbers within lines on a page, these books allow falling writers to just write, without having to focus on the lines. You will want to have them trace over dotted letters while simultaneously verbalizing the letter-formation command *as* they write. For example, a lowercase *a* would be written while saying, "Around, up, down." Have students repeat this procedure many times on unlined paper. Students can write sentences and stories in their unlined books, and you will want to encourage them to write their letters smaller as they become more proficient with formation.

2. Students love paper-plate books! You can punch one hole through four or five plates and tie a small piece of yarn through the hole. Now, students can color the ridges of the plate and write their words and sentences in the center space. Plastic-coated paper plates offer a nice surface that supports the formation of letters smoothly, quickly, and easily, using a fine-line marker. Paper-plate books can also be laminated after writers complete their stories. They are cheap and motivating!

THINKING IT OVER

Why do we teach children to form their letters within small lines? What are the benefits of that, and do these benefits apply to *all* writers in your class? When is the right time to insist that students use lined paper and form letters legibly within those lines?

15

Catch a Falling
Writer by . . .

Teaching Proper Penmanship Positions

There are proper positions for playing the violin, typing on a keyboard, and hitting a golf ball. The same is true for writing.

There are proper positions for playing the violin, typing on a keyboard, and hitting a golf ball. The same is true for writing.

Many students are unaware of the proper way to position themselves when they write. The results are sloppy work, tired hands, and sore backs. If you look around the room while children are writing, you will notice a wide range of positions. Some of them are naturally engaged in a proper penmanship position, while others are not.

Consider the following points:

IMPORTANT TO KNOW

1. As teachers, we might assume that our students come to us knowing how to sit properly and how to write legibly. However, that is not always the case, especially with falling writers. We can't assume anything, no matter what grade level these children are in!

2. If you see a writer using an improper head position (with the head down low and the face close to the paper), contact the parent to recommend that the child be given an eye exam. You need your eyes to read and write! Improper head positions can be an indicator that students need glasses when they read and write.

3. When students are asked what a proper penmanship position is, most will tell you they don't know. I would argue that many of them do know and are using it already, but they have rarely been asked the question, so they have never really thought about it. Most falling writers, however, simply don't know and don't engage in a beneficial position for writing.

SOLUTIONS

1. Children need to be taught the proper way to position themselves for writing. These are the instructions that need to be given as a reminder of the proper handwriting position:
   o Sit up straight and tall.
   o Place both feet flat on the floor.
   o Move your chair close to the desk without squishing your stomach.
   o Tilt your paper slightly away from the hand you write with, and hold the corner of it with the hand you don't write with.
   o Place your writing arm, up to your elbow, on the desk as you write. This will keep your hand and wrist from getting tired because it will be supported by your arm.
   o Relax your shoulders, and look up once in a while to give your eyes a rest.

2. Model this position often for students. I highly recommend that you also model what *not* to do. For example, show them a position where you hold your head with your left hand, stick your right leg out to the side of the desk, and lower your head close to the paper. They will laugh, but they will learn from your example of what not to do!

THINKING IT OVER

Why do we need to teach children how to position themselves for writing when it seems like such an obvious thing? Do the size and height of classroom tables and desks matter? Hmmm . . .

16

Catch a Falling
Writer by . . .

Attending to Directionality and Spacing

Why should I do it "this way"?

Why do some writers start from the right and go left? Why do some of them write their first sentence on the bottom and their second and third sentences above it instead of below it? Why do many children write a "string of letters" and forget to put spaces between words? These are questions that all of us have asked ourselves at one time or another.

Consider the following points:

IMPORTANT TO KNOW

1. Many falling writers are just too busy thinking of what to write, how to form their letters, and which sounds they hear in words to worry about directionality and spacing.

2. Some students perceive that writing something from right to left is the way it should be done. It may be that the children have not been following text as someone read to them. Also, it may be that the children are simply not reading enough to notice the way print goes. Finally, for some writers, it may be an indicator of visual-perceptual problems, and if it persists, you may decide to refer them for testing in this area.

3. Voice-print match takes time and experience with print. When students have limited prior knowledge of how print works, they often write words in a string, without spaces between them. We need to teach them why the spaces are necessary.

SOLUTIONS

1. Place a large green dot where the writer should start writing and a large red dot at the far right where the writer should stop. Do the same for lines that follow. Repeat this procedure for all written work (on unlined or lined paper) until you see a shift in her understanding of directionality. Have the child point to each dot and say, "Start, stop," until she can write correctly from left to right without the colored dots.

2. When a falling writer composes a sentence or phrase using a string of letters, simply take the pencil or marker and write the same thing below the original sentence. Then, ask the child to read both sentences. After that, say, "Which one was easier to read? Why?" It is inevitable that the child will pick yours. Now, have the student rewrite the sentence (using spaces in between words) and read it back to you once more. Each time the child writes in a string of letters, try this procedure until the child understands the role of spacing between words.

THINKING IT OVER

There are many ways of addressing directionality and spacing issues for writers. The solutions above are the ones I found to be most effective in the shortest amount of time. What are other ways of attending to these two critical issues? You may want to discuss these with your colleagues. Teachers of students with special needs and occupational therapists have all kinds of tools in their toolboxes!

17

Catch a Falling Writer by . . .

Correcting Errors

If you let me think that it is right, I may never learn that it is wrong.

In an attempt to preserve feelings of self-confidence and self-worth in children, people shy away from correcting student's errors. This reluctance is based on a flawed concept, and what it actually does is rob children of the skills necessary to recognize when something is wrong and fix it. If we give falling writers a false sense of pride, they may enjoy writing for a while, but eventually they will come to hate it. They will learn quickly that their writing is not up to grade-level standards.

Consider the following points:

IMPORTANT TO KNOW

1. When young children are first learning to write, it is important that we just let them write! They will ask us how to spell words, and we will encourage them to write what they

hear. They will ask us if their attempts are correct, and instead of telling them they are correct, we will help them fix them.

2. Rule of thumb: On any word that is considered a sight word (a word that is used repetitively), praise writers for their attempt, and show them what it really looks like. Have them write the word correctly, copying yours for accuracy.

3. When falling writers ask if they wrote something correctly, they truly want to know! Tell them the truth.

SOLUTIONS

1. White correction tape is a great tool to have on hand for covering up a child's errors and for writing corrections on top of the tape. It prevents the writer's work from looking marked up and offers a simple solution that is better than erasing or starting over.

2. All writers need praise and encouragement, because writing is hard work! Falling writers need extra doses of validation and then correction, so they can begin to self-monitor their own writing. For example, a student writes:

My Mom sez that pizza is good and for you.

As the teacher or parent, I would do and say the following:
"Good sentence. Now please read it back for me."
"Does it make sense?" If the child answers, "Yes," I would say, "We don't say it that way. We say something is good for you. What do you need to do to fix your sentence? Here is some correction tape. What do you have to cover so it all makes sense?"
"Good for you for hearing the sounds in the word *says*. It does sound like there should be an *e* and a *z*, doesn't it? Now let me show you what it really looks like." Write the word correctly on a whiteboard or scrap paper. Have the student write it several times before correcting the original sentence with tape. You may have the student put the word *says* on an index card to file in a word bank for future use. It is a common word.

THINKING IT OVER

Can we help falling students feel confident and pleased with their writing while also empowering them with essential corrections? What message are we sending about the process of editing one's work if we don't do this from a young age?

18

Catch a Falling
Writer by . . .

Articulating Words Aloud

Try writing "Supercalifragulisticexpealidocious" as fast as you can, without moving your lips or bobbing your head.

Try writing *Supercalifragilisticexpialidocious* as fast as you can, without moving your lips or bobbing your head.

When we spell a new or difficult word, we almost always say the word aloud and move our head, so we can hear the sounds and syllables within the word. Even adults do that on unfamiliar words they are trying to spell. Watch falling writers write. Nothing comes out of their mouths. In fact, the lips of falling writers rarely ever move, and their heads don't bob when they are writing a word they don't know. Their brains are simply not telling them to do these things. Consider the following points:

IMPORTANT TO KNOW

1. The act of verbalizing a word aloud is a natural one for many writers. It just feels right, almost as if we are saying it to our ears! This is what good writers and spellers do. This is what falling writers need to be taught to do.

2. Many falling writers have trouble counting syllables. It feels unnatural to them to move their heads up and down while saying a word in an effort to hear the parts within the word. They must be taught to do this.

3. Good diction has everything to do with spelling new words correctly. If a student is saying *Mother* with a *d* sound in the middle, that's exactly what the student will write: *Moder.* How we pronounce words makes a difference in how we spell them, especially for falling writers.

SOLUTIONS

1. Pretend that you are Jiminy Cricket, sitting on the shoulder of a falling writer. While standing behind the student, ask him to say the word aloud *as* he writes the word. You will have to be insistent here. Many children just do not like to do it, but once they see how it will help them, they start to move their lips and "whisper" the word to their ears.

2. As you teach falling writers how to articulate words aloud, be sure to teach them to move their heads to the natural rhythm of the word. In other words, you are teaching them to count syllables with their head while saying the word slowly. You will also want to model how to stretch the word slowly, so they can hear all the sounds within the word, not just some of them. Pronouncing the word correctly is vitally important.

THINKING IT OVER

When I ask children if it is all right with their teacher if they say words aloud, softly, while they write, they tell me, "No!" Their teachers are usually shocked by this. Do your students know that it's OK to say words aloud as they write? Ask them. You may be surprised to see how many falling writers don't know it is perfectly fine with you.

19

Catch a Falling
Writer by . . .

Tapping, Stomping, and Jumping Words

We teach kids to stop, drop, and roll. Sometimes we just have to stop and tap, stomp, and jump!

We teach students to stop, drop, and roll. Sometimes we just have to tap, stomp, and jump!

Words are made up of syllables, and knowing how to break up a word into syllables is valuable. Too many students today can't identify how many syllables exist within a word. As I observe students around the country with this problem, I have concluded that many of them simply aren't pronouncing words accurately. If you don't say it correctly, how will you hear the parts within it correctly?

Consider the following points:

IMPORTANT TO KNOW

1. Teaching children to syllabicate should be done as early as preschool. Waiting until second and third grade is too late. It poses problems for writers because they have trouble

hearing isolated parts within words as they write them. They might say long, hard words aloud, but they don't hear the parts, so they often write the first part and the last part of the word.

2. Most children have difficulty identifying one-syllable words. They say *Ju-ump* and bob their heads up and down twice, instead of once.

3. Even if students can correctly identify syllables within a word, they may not be pronouncing the word correctly. Pronunciation and diction matter. Correct them on their pronunciation and emphasize good, clear diction throughout the day.

SOLUTIONS

1. You can model how to hear syllables within words by saying the word aloud slowly while doing the following:

   o Tap each syllable with your hand on the table.
   o Stomp each syllable with your foot on the floor.
   o Stand up and jump each syllable with your body.
   o Count each syllable with your fingers.
   o Move your head up and down for each syllable.
   o Blink your eyes for each syllable.
   o Clap your hands for each syllable.

2. After you teach children how to count syllables in words, assess them by having them hold up a *yes* or *no* card as you pronounce different words for them. For instance, say *refrigerator* aloud while jumping only three times. See who holds up a *yes* and who holds up a *no.* Most falling writers need several lessons on this before they can independently identify syllables within words.

THINKING IT OVER

Do your students know *why* they need to be able to say and count syllables within words? Do they buy into *how* this strategy will help them when they spell new and difficult words? Teach them to tap, stomp, and jump!

20

Catch a Falling
Writer by . . .

Practicing Letter Formations and Sight Words

When we first learned to drive, we had to think about every action. With practice, most actions became automatic.

When we first learned to drive, we had to think about every action. With practice, most actions became automatic.

Those of us who teach know that practice makes perfect. It is a timeless principle that we would be wise never to forget. Falling writers need to practice proper letter formation and sight words until they become automatic. Once this happens, they can focus their attention on other things like spelling hard words, writing complete sentences, connecting their thoughts, and editing their work.

Consider the following points:

IMPORTANT TO KNOW

1. If children learn to write their name and other basic sight words using uppercase (capital) letters only, they have a

difficult time relearning them using lowercase letters. Most words are written with lowercase letter formations. Teach young writers those first!

2. When falling writers are allowed to write letters in unusual ways, they commit these to their long-term memory. Behaviors that become habitual are very hard to break, especially during times of stress and pressure. They need to know that an *o* goes to the left, not to the right.

3. Sight words must be spelled correctly from the very beginning. Too many children go to upper grades writing *very* as *vere*, *which* as *wich*, and *was* as *wuz*. Requiring them to spell sight words correctly, from the beginning, is a gift.

SOLUTIONS

1. Group letters and numbers together by common formations. For instance, teach students formations of all the letters that start with a stick: *b, h, k, l, p, r, u, v, w, x, y*. As they write these letters, be sure that they are verbalizing the command, so their brains connect the words with the motion: "Down, up, and around." "Down." "Down, up." "Down, down." This is the *best* way to teach struggling writers to form their letters properly and, more important, to commit them to memory. The more they write them, the more automatic they will become. Have them trace over dotted letters five times and then practice them on their own five times. Do this daily for several weeks, and they will learn their letters and numbers correctly, both in uppercase and lowercase.

2. Sight words need to be brought to fluency. That means the falling writers need to write them over and over again, correctly. Writing them and erasing them on a whiteboard is effective. Writing them in each corner of a blank sheet of paper is also fast and fun. Writing them with their pointer finger in the dust on the chalkboard is different and motivating. Practicing them with a wet paintbrush on a dark sheet of construction paper is also motivating and "magical." There are many sight-word lists. If every teacher in your building does not have a list of common sight words to use, speak to the leaders in your school immediately!

THINKING IT OVER

How can we educate parents about the importance of proper upper- and lowercase letter formations and the need for sight-word automaticity? Can these issues be addressed during school open houses and parent-teacher conferences? If so, what is the most effective way of sharing this information with parents, especially parents or guardians of falling writers?

21

Catch a Falling
Writer by . . .

Rebuilding Cut-Up Sentences

Sometimes we have to take things apart to put them back together again.

The idea of copying a student's sentence onto a strip of poster board and cutting it up is not new. It is a technique that should be used only with those who struggle. Not all kids benefit from rebuilding cut-up words and sounds within words. They simply don't need to do that. Falling writers, on the other hand, can benefit from this powerful technique.

Consider the following points:

IMPORTANT TO KNOW

1. Cut-up sentences serve to teach students how words work within a complete sentence. They can also teach children to verbalize sounds within words and check to see if their attempts make sense and look right. This is important for self-monitoring and independence.

2. When writers rebuild a sentence that they have written, they are forced to use problem-solving skills and to direct their attention to details. This tends to increase attention span, and we know that many falling kids have short attention spans for a variety of reasons.

3. As students become more and more successful at rebuilding cut-up sentences, they begin to really think about sounds within words, syllables, and conventional writing standards (upper- and lowercase usage, punctuation, directionality, spacing, etc.) and they will then apply these *as* they write.

SOLUTIONS

1. Using a dark marker, write the student's sentence correctly on a one-inch strip of oak tag or poster board. As you cut it up, you will want to consider the needs of the individual, so you will cut accordingly. For instance, a young child who has difficulty using spaces between words will need to have sentences cut between the words only. Falling writers who have difficulty hearing ending sounds, blends, vowel combinations, or syllables within words will need to have sentences cut with these things in mind. Do not be afraid to raise the level of difficulty as students get used to problem solving their cut-up sentences. Encourage them to verbalize the words *as* they rebuild their sentence, and always remind them to read it over to see if it makes sense and looks right before they tape their sentence onto a sheet of paper or chart paper. If it doesn't, they will need to fix it!

2. After students have rebuilt their sentence and checked it for accuracy, rearrange the cut-up sentence in different ways, so they read it back in different ways. This procedure builds fluency and visual tracking skills. *Note:* It is *very* important that you model how to do this, teaching children to put their words together like they talk. The student must read each phrase back *without stopping between words*. This will take time and practice, but you will see a shift in the student's reading fluency. This will also help falling writers to create sentences that are rich in

descriptive phrases and to use more than just a few words per sentence.

For example, the rebuilt sentence is

I am very good at playing baseball and like it more than soccer.

I might rearrange the words as follows:

I am very
good at playing baseball
and like it more
than soccer.

After the student reads it back the way I arranged it, I might rearrange it again, maintaining fluent phrasing, so their eyes are forced to read it in a different way:

I am very good at
playing baseball and like it
more than
soccer.

I would rearrange it one more time to move the eyes across the lines even farther:

I am very good
at playing baseball and like it
more than soccer.

THINKING IT OVER

How long do we continue practicing with struggling students? If we decide that they have mastered certain intervention strategies such as the cut-up sentence, do we give ourselves permission to revisit these with students in the future? Sometimes a baby needs to go back to crawling in order to walk, yes?

Part III

Creating Independence

This final part of the book is designed to give teachers and parents a variety of strategies for creating independence in falling writers. You might ask why this is important. The bottom line is that we must gradually release responsibility to children, so they will be empowered to complete tasks without a lot of prompting, assistance, and motivation. We want our falling writers to feel self-confident in their ability to communicate through the written word, and we want them to be motivated from within. If they believe they can read, write, and think successfully, they will be able to handle any task or assignment they are presented as they progress through the grade levels. The greatest gifts we can give children are roots and wings. When we create independence in falling writers, we are on our way to helping them fly on their own!

In this part, we will focus on the following areas:

Catch a Falling Writer by . . . *Using Verbal Prompts for Self-Editing*

Catch a Falling Writer by . . . *Offering a Pinch of Praise*

Catch a Falling Writer by . . . *Recording Oral Responses on Sticky Notes*

Catch a Falling Writer by . . . *Offering a Variety of Focus Sheets*

Catch a Falling Writer by . . . *Dealing With Procrastination*

Catch a Falling Writer by . . . *Using a Variety of "Good" Questions*

Catch a Falling Writer by . . . *Adding Art, Music, and Drama*

Catch a Falling Writer by . . . *Connecting Writing With Reading*

Catch a Falling Writer by . . . *Guiding Writers in Small-Group Instruction*

22

Catch a Falling Writer by . . .

Using Verbal Prompts for Self-Editing

It is the writer, not the teacher or parent, who is ultimately responsible for editing his or her own piece of writing.

If asked to define true north, in terms of where we are going with falling writers, what would that definition be? One definition might be that we are trying to help young writers finish their assignments as their peers do. Another might define it as a set of tools we give all writers. Still another definition might focus on getting students to respond to assignments with relative ease and comfort. The truth is that all of these definitions are acceptable outcomes for catching falling writers, but true north should be defined as follows: *Every falling writer must be able to write on grade level, independently.* The meaning of *on grade level* is subjective to the school standards within the population of that school, but the key word in this definition is *independently.* Without independence, students are left with a bunch of tools and strategies in a toolbox that has to be opened or supported by someone else.

The secret to achieving true north for falling writers is to empower each one with a set of internal verbal prompts that helps them edit their work independently as they go along. Please read that again! If children rely on others to assist them in thinking of what to write, where to write it, how to spell words, how to fix errors, when to add more, where to go for information, and how to rewrite an initial draft, they will most likely resort to writing the simplest stories possible so that none of this occurs. If you are reading this, then you know kids who do that!

If we want to instill verbal prompts in falling kids, we must offer them consistently and frequently until we see evidence that they have become *internalized* within the writer's thinking processes. Here are several prompts that can be either written or used orally to move students towards independence in their writing:

> ➢ Who am I writing this story for?
> ➢ What will a reader learn from reading my story?
> ➢ Does it make sense?
> ➢ Does it "look" right?
> ➢ How can I fix misspelled words?
> ➢ What else can I add?
> ➢ Is my story "thick" or "thin"?
> ➢ Did I forget anything?

You may think that a student would need many more prompts than the eight listed above. However, think again. Each one of these is "loaded" with strategies that need to be taught in order to answer them. For example, students need to know whom they are being asked to write for, even if it is just for themselves. There must be an intention for the assignment, or it becomes meaningless and frivolous. Another example of a loaded prompt is "Does it look right?" Students must be taught *how* to check their writing in order to edit it properly. At first, you may want to give them a checklist of things to look for, such as proper capital letter usage, periods, spacing, left to right directionality, and spelling.

Most writing curriculums and language-arts programs introduce these strategies at the kindergarten level, and they are reinforced throughout the grade levels; however, many falling writers fail to internalize these. They simply do not know what to do when asked, "Does it look right?" This is where the teacher must define these prompts for students and be sure that they are using learned strategies when prompted to take action. Otherwise, the prompts merely become something that the teachers or parents ask and not something the students ask themselves.

The purpose of verbal prompting is to achieve independence, or true north, so that kids can write, edit, revise, and publish their work without adult intervention. After all, no one will be standing over them in middle school and high school, and we certainly do not want them to rely solely on a computer to correct spelling and grammar errors. A computer can certainly help, but it cannot replace the power of the writer. Every writer must have the ability to shape the written word into a masterpiece independently of anyone or anything else. Otherwise, why teach kids to write?

23

Catch a Falling
Writer by . . .

Offering a Pinch
of Praise

*If you want to make most things taste good, add a pinch of
salt or sugar. If you want to help a falling writer, add a pinch
of praise.*

Praise is a funny thing because if we give too much, it loses its
value and power. If we give too little, it fails to serve as a cata-
lyst for motivation and pride. Falling writers benefit most from
praise that is "just right" and meaningful. The whole purpose for
praise is to help individuals judge whether their work is on target or
not. Otherwise, anything goes, and everything would be accepted
as grade-level writing. We live in a society where there are standards, and without some measure by which we can analyze our
own work, we have no way of knowing if we are doing what is
expected or not.

The best way to get good at offering praise is to develop a
repertoire of phrases and behaviors similar to what a spice rack
might have. One has oregano, basil, and parsley for most Italian
dishes and cinnamon, nutmeg, and allspice for many desserts!

Similarly, we want to accumulate verbal and written phrases for praising falling kids while also developing a sense of the way we deliver praise through our behaviors.

Let's start with a list of things we might actually say to writers as they are writing:

(*Note:* These could also be written on a child's paper or story if it is a more appropriate form of praise, depending on the circumstances for offering feedback.)

> ➢ "I like the way you stopped and really thought about what comes next in your story."
> ➢ "Good. . . . You are thinking and writing at the same time!"
> ➢ "You went back and read it over to see if it makes sense. That's what good writers do!"
> ➢ "I like the way you fixed that. Good writers fix things along the way."
> ➢ "Super job of remembering to put an uppercase letter at the beginning of each sentence."
> ➢ "Good for you! You are thinking about where to put the punctuation marks in your story."
> ➢ "You are really focusing on doing your best writing. Keep going!"
> ➢ "I am amazed at the way you are really thinking about what you are writing. Keep thinking!"
> ➢ "Nice! You underlined words that didn't look right to you on your first draft. Now what will you do to fix those?"
> ➢ "Good writers reread their stories to see if they make sense. I noticed that you did that. Good for you!"
> ➢ "You did what good writers do when they get stuck. You stopped to think about what you have already and what more you need."
> ➢ "I am so impressed that you asked yourself what else you could do to make your writing better! All good writers do that. Keep it up!"

You may wish to add your own:

_____

_____

_____

Now, let's examine our own behaviors for delivering praise, both orally and in writing. This is an important step to catch falling writers. We must praise them in ways that help them internalize writing strategies, so they will employ them on a regular basis. Otherwise, what good is praise and constructive feedback? It is the writer who must be able to ultimately praise herself, and we can help this along by examining *how* we deliver praise to those who fall. Here are some reflective questions you may want to ask yourself when working with struggling writers:

> ➤ What am I physically doing when I praise kids?
> ➤ Am I standing directly in front of the student? Am I looking down on him?
> ➤ Am I sitting across from the student engaging in eye contact as I praise her?
> ➤ Am I standing behind the student whispering into his ear?
> ➤ Am I pointing to a specific part of their writing that I am praising them about?
> ➤ What is the child's physical reaction to my praise?
> ➤ What is the tone in my voice? Is it effective, and how do I know?
> ➤ How is the volume and pitch of my voice when I am delivering praise?
> ➤ If I am praising her in writing, what color pen am I using?
> ➤ Where have I written the praise, for example, at the top of the page, in the side margins, directly above or below the child's writing, at the bottom of the page, or at the end of the story?
> ➤ Knowing this particular child, what is the best way to deliver praise?
> ➤ What can I do to give praise and simultaneously work to create independence within the falling writer?
> ➤ How is my attempt to praise this child going to actually help him become a more self-sufficient writer?
> ➤ What does this individual need from me in terms of praise and constructive feedback? Should I say it or write it?
> ➤ How often does this student need praise when writing, and how do I know this?

Offering praise is nowhere near as easy as adding a pinch of salt or sugar to something we are cooking! It requires reflection, practice, more practice, trial and error, and student feedback to know if what we are offering actually works. The tricky thing is that the type of praise and the amount of praise that work for one child may not work for another child. It is what some might call the craft of teaching, and it is not easy, but it is essential for catching falling kids. Keep at it until you find just the right pinch of praise for each and every falling writer you work with.

24

Catch a Falling
Writer by . . .

Recording Oral Responses on Sticky Notes

The one who created sticky notes probably had no clue they would be so valuable to teachers and kids!

U nlike a highlighter, a sticky note is a response tool that can be used effectively to link reading, writing, and thinking, without ruining the book! Its uses are varied and flexible, depending on the purpose of the activity. In the case of falling writers, it is best to initially model the ways in which one can use a sticky note. You might show the kids how to write a question on it *as* they read or how to mark a page and then return to it to record some thoughts. Teachers and parents who model the way in which we use a tool are more likely to be the ones who see kids using such tools as they write. If a teacher writes questions or unknown words on sticky notes and attaches them to a book that he is reading aloud, students will want to do the same. The teacher is walking the talk, and kids will most likely do the same.

There are several advantages to having falling writers use sticky notes, as opposed to whiteboards or writing journals, during small-group reading lessons:

- Sticky notes have no lines, and falling writers like this. They can just write without thinking about whether their letters need to touch the top, middle, or bottom line.
- Sticky notes encourage more legible writing because they are small in size. They simply can't hold a lot of big letters and numbers!
- Sticky notes can be attached to books without marking or tearing pages.
- Sticky notes can be numbered and saved in manila folders or on poster board for easy rereading and completion.
- Sticky notes come in various shapes, colors, and sizes. Kids like to have options!
- Sticky notes are inexpensive and easy to store.
- Sticky notes can be placed anywhere on a page, depending on the purpose for using them.

Consider using sticky notes with wordless picture books, so falling writers can write a sentence or two to go with each picture. Offer sticky notes to students who need practice identifying things such as facts, opinions, new words, funny lines, and so forth. I recommend that students not only place the sticky note next to the section or page they are asked to identify, but also write down the answer on the sticky note. This reinforces two things: (1) They did, in fact, identify the correct thing they were searching for, and (2) they get practice in writing down the response, even if they copy it.

Finally, you can use sticky notes effectively when setting a purpose for reading by asking students to write down what they found out on the note and then stick it on the edge of the page where they found the answer. For example, you might say, "Read until you figure out how the boy found his lost dog" or "Write your answer on a sticky note and post it on the page that helped you figure out that problem."

Sticky notes are worthwhile and useful. Put them on your classroom wish list. My guess is that even Santa uses them to jot down a few reminders during the month of December!

25

Catch a Falling Writer by . . .

Offering a Variety of Focus Sheets

A focus sheet does for kids what a calendar does for adults.

A focus sheet is another tool to use with writers to help them focus their ideas, thoughts, and purposes for writing. It is short and sweet! It is most often attached to a clipboard so that kids can write on it as they read. While it is a way to "get started" on a writing assignment, it also serves as a tool for bridging reading, writing, and thinking in a small-group setting.

Focus sheets are similar to graphic organizers, but they tend to be more creative and less structured. Quite simply, I think of a focus sheet as a way to help build critical-thinking skills in my students without requiring a lot of writing from them. Remember, focus sheets are effective and efficient!

You will want to create your own focus sheets depending on your unique purposes for using them, especially with falling writers, but the next two pages provide two to get you started (see "Appendix: Focus Sheets" for additional focus sheets).

FOCUS SHEET

Predictions

Write down one idea you'd like to investigate after you read:

_____

_____

_____

_____

_____

_____

_____

_____

_____

_____

As you read, jot down one or two questions that come to your mind:

_____

_____

_____

_____

_____

_____

_____

_____

_____

_____

_____

FOCUS SHEET

Vocabulary

List any words that are unusual or "tricky" for you:

26

Catch a Falling Writer by . . .

Dealing With Procrastination

If you don't think you can do something well, why do it at all?

Falling writers like to procrastinate. It's a fact of life that most of us come to know if we teach long enough. If given a choice of whether to write in a daily journal or not, most would choose not to for a variety of reasons that we will consider. The important point here is that when readers and writers procrastinate, this is a sign that something is probably difficult or tedious for them. If it weren't, there would be no need to procrastinate, right?

Consider the mind-sets of many falling writers. They know they have to write in their journals or complete a writing assignment for seatwork, but they do everything possible to delay these tasks. In case you are too busy teaching to notice these delay tactics, here is a list of behaviors that you might see if you were a fly on the wall, watching a group of falling writers!

- Searching for a pencil
- Sharpening a pencil

- Dropping a pencil (several times!)
- Writing, erasing, tearing paper, starting over
- Playing with things on or near the desk
- Walking around the room looking busy
- Chatting with a friend
- Writing, erasing, tearing paper, starting over
- Searching for paper or a journal
- Going to the bathroom
- Getting a drink of water
- Writing, erasing, tearing paper, starting over
- Asking a neighbor (or two!) what the assignment is
- Asking several people how to spell words
- Coughing, laughing, or re-sharpening a pencil
- Writing, erasing, tearing paper, starting over (again!)

These behaviors are real and frequent, as all experienced teachers recognize. If you study the behaviors just listed, you will notice a lot of starting, stopping, and starting over again. This is not good, because it disturbs the natural process of writing and causes the student to experience the sense of failure.

There are three main reasons why falling readers engage in these behaviors when they are asked to write:

1. Falling writers don't feel like successful writers.

2. Falling writers don't have enough tools in their writer's toolbox.

3. Falling writers can't think of something to write.

Let's try to understand each of these reasons better, so we can move to eliminate them from the mind-set of a falling writer. A feeling of success comes when one feels as though one has done something well. It comes only from within, and no one can create that feeling for you. It acts as an intrinsic motivator that keeps us from giving up. If a writer knows that she has fallen behind (or if the act of writing is slow and tedious), she doesn't develop a feeling of success. This leads to procrastination, and on and on it goes.

We can help falling writers realize a sense of success by starting with what they know in order to get to somewhere new. Let me repeat that: Start with what they know. If they know how to write only one word, start with that word and build the assignment around it. It's something they know and can write easily. Simultaneously, you will want to increase their storehouse of written words by having them write basic sight words *daily*. They should write a common word, erase it, write it, erase it, write it, erase it, and so forth. This will bring an assortment of new words to fluency, so they can use them to achieve successful results in their written responses and stories.

We have looked at a number of tools that are necessary for writers who struggle. Among those mentioned are webs, picture files, dictionaries, alphabet charts, fine-line markers, white correction tape, sticky notes, paper-plate books, and other kinds of unlined paper. Without a variety of tools at their disposal, falling writers tend to just "sit there." After they have access to a good variety of tools, if they are still sitting there, then perhaps the issue is not a lack of tools. Perhaps they are distracted because of where they are sitting or who they are sitting near. Perhaps they do not know that they can get up to go to the writing center to retrieve tools they need. Perhaps they simply don't understand what they are expected to do.

This leads to the third reason: They can't think of something to write. This is very common among falling writers, and it becomes a great excuse for them to use. One of the reasons they use it is because it makes sense and people buy it. If you can't think of something to write, how can you possibly write? Problem solved. But this is unacceptable thinking, so we must help these writers move away from this excuse and into a possibility frame of mind.

The best suggestion I have to help the student overcome this stumbling block is to offer choices. When students have choices, they feel more invested because they can apply what they know to something they feel they had a choice in selecting. For example, if the daily assignment is to write each spelling word in a complete sentence, one will definitely lose the interest of students. It's boring, predictable, and tedious. A better way is to offer three choices: (1) Select any five spelling words that you want, and write each one in a sentence; (2) take each spelling word, look it up in the dictionary, and write the page number you found it on next to the word; or (3) draw a picture of five of your spelling words, and then write an "I think . . ." sentence under each picture.

Now watch what happens to the excuse "I can't think of any-thing to write." They have choices, and these are all centered on using their spelling words in meaningful ways. Other choices for free-writing activities might look something like these: (1) Choose a wordless book. Read the pictures, and write a sentence to go with three of the pictures. (2) Find three pictures in the picture file. Make up a newspaper story that has to do with all three pictures. (3) Think of someone famous whom you would like to inter-view. Write three questions you would ask this person.

We can work toward creating a feeling of success by helping falling writers utilize a good selection of tools. They will feel empowered to write something they had a choice in, and we will see greater independence. The main thing is to keep the writing train moving daily without all the stopping, starting, and excuses. Choo-choo!

27

Catch a Falling
Writer by . . .

Using a Variety of "Good" Questions

Good thinkers continually ask themselves good questions.

O ne of the best practices educators and parents can engage in is to reflect on the kinds of questions we ask children daily. Different kinds of questions require different kinds of thinking. Therefore, if we agree that writing is really just thinking brought down to the pen, then we would be wise to create independent thinkers. This difficult task is most effectively accomplished by asking "good" questions.

Many of us are surprised to learn that our tendency is to ask more yes or no questions than any other kind. A yes or no question is simply a question that requires a *yes* or a *no* answer. It does not require much thought, it is quick and easy to come up with, and there is usually a right or wrong to it. Why do you suppose yes or no questions are asked more than any other type? Quite simply, the reason is *time.* We often feel so pressured to cover so much material in such a short amount of time with a whole class of kids that we resort to the fastest way of making sure they understand.

This is certainly understandable, and there is nothing wrong with asking a yes or no question, occasionally. The problem comes in when we ask them almost all the time, because this greatly limits a child's ability to think critically and to respond with more than just one word.

So, what do we do about this problem? First, we need to examine the kinds of questions we ask to determine if there is a problem. In other words, if you already ask a wide range of questions on a daily basis, then you are probably already aware of the importance of this. If you are not sure whether you do or not, just keep a log for one or two days. I suggest writing down every question you ask *after* you ask it. At the end of the day, review your questions by counting how many yes or no questions you have versus other kinds. Reflect on the results, and see if you need to become more aware of how you question kids, particularly falling writers. Be especially aware of the kinds of questions you ask students who use English as a second language and students with special needs; the tendency is to modify questions to the point where they are not given enough opportunity to think and respond beyond yes and no thinking.

Once you have taken time to reflect on your own questioning skills, you will want to consider using a variety of questions. There are lots of professional books out there on building comprehension through "good questioning" (see "Recommended Web Sites, Research, and Texts"), but many suggestions require advance planning. Planning our questions is important and necessary, but we often find ourselves asking questions during times when we are not in the midst of a lesson (i.e., during morning meeting discussions, while engaging in reading aloud, during show-and-tell times, while waiting in class lines, or during lunch). These are the times when being able to formulate good questions, on the run, is very valuable.

Here are six guidelines for asking questions. If you practice following all six of them daily, asking a variety of questions will become automatic. You will be asking good questions while "on the run" with your falling writers.

1. Ask questions that require kids to *solve* a problem.

2. Ask questions that make kids *connect* one thing to another.

3. Ask questions that use the *senses.*

4. Ask questions that require *inference.*

5. Ask questions that force an *evaluation* of some kind.

6. Ask questions that tap into a child's *memory* bank.

Here are key words from all six guidelines (Suggestion: Write them in the palm of your hand or on an index card!):

1. Solve

2. Connect

3. Sense

4. Infer

5. Evaluate

6. Remember

Below are sample questions I might ask kids while in line for physical education class:

➤ What could we do if we wanted to score more baskets in a basketball game? (Solve)
➤ Can anyone tell us what volleyball and soccer have in common? (Connect)
➤ If you had to describe what a baseball game is like to someone who is blind, what would you tell them? (Sense)
➤ Who can tell us why a basketball might get stuck in the hoop? (Infer)
➤ What is the worst thing you can do if you are a player on a team? (Evaluate)
➤ How do you count points if you are bowling? (Remember)

These questions not only lead your students to higher levels of thinking, they also provide a springboard of ideas for your next journal-writing assignment!

If asking good questions produces better writers and thinkers, then why not get good at it and see what happens? *All* kids deserve more than *yes* or *no* questions. Yes!

28

Catch a Falling
Writer by . . .

Adding Art, Music, and Drama

We use a tool to draw, a voice to sing, and expressions to act.
Sounds like what we do when we write!

I think we can all agree that art, music, and drama are universal languages. No matter where we grow up or what culture we are born into, we can find these languages in our ancestry. They are like threads used to connect patches of a quilt. They transcend differences and offer ways of expressing ourselves without boundaries or limitations. Falling writers often make friends with art, music, and drama for these very reasons. They can express their thoughts without all the conventions that accompany the written word.

Knowing this can help us to use art, music, and drama as a way of teaching kids to take risks with expression. If they are good at drawing, they can draw first, and then write. If they like music, they can sing a song and write more lyrics or write new words to a favorite tune. If they enjoy drama, they can write a script for Reader's Theater. The trick is to find out which universal language they are most connected to and use it as a "hook."

Here are a few hooks you might try:

➤ Paint a picture, and write five words at the bottom to describe what you see when you look at it.
➤ Do a scribble creature and give it a name. Write a story with your scribble creature as the main character. Add other scribble creatures to make your story even more interesting.
➤ Draw a new cover for your favorite story. Write three sentences on the back cover to let someone know what the story is about.
➤ Change all the words to your favorite song. How would it go? Write them down; then sing it to someone!
➤ Think of a song that makes you feel proud. Write about why this song makes you feel that way.
➤ Tap out the rhythm to a song that you know by heart. Now, write a new word for each tap, and then perform it for somebody.
➤ Draw three faces, and paste each one onto a small wooden stick. These are your puppets. Each of your puppets has a problem. Write down what each puppet's problem is. Now, write what they would say to each other to solve all three problems. Act it out, using the lines you wrote for your puppets.
➤ Write a script about a favorite fairy tale. You are the writer, so you may change it any way you would like to. Be sure to include several characters, so you and some friends can perform it. Don't forget to reread it to see if it makes sense and looks right. Actors need good scripts!

Art, music, and drama are powerful tools for encouraging writing in many different ways. Draw a little, sing a little, act a little, and write a lot! That sounds like a new song, doesn't it?

29

Catch a Falling Writer by . . .

Connecting Writing With Reading

What I can write, I can read.

If you were taught to include writing within your small-group reading instruction, go back and thank your instructors! Most of us were not taught this. Reading groups were about reading. Writing was mainly done as a separate assignment for seatwork, as a journal response for writer's workshop, or as a homework assignment. We rarely see opportunities for writing to occur within the structure of a reading group, and this is unfortunate. Reading groups afford teachable moments that can be used to strengthen the connection between reading and writing.

Many falling writers are fairly good readers. But you won't find fairly good writers who are poor readers. It simply doesn't work that way! With this in mind, consider the knowledge gained from analysis of a child's writing behaviors and written work. If we want to know what children need in reading, analyze their writing. The more we connect reading and writing for kids, the faster they will progress in both areas.

The best way to connect writing with reading is to try not to separate them. Here are some suggestions for keeping the reading and writing connection alive and well in your classroom:

> ➤ Be sure to have plenty of things for kids to *read* in your *writing* center, such as alphabet charts, idea cards, sight-word phrases, dictionaries, suggested titles, open-ended sentences on strips, wordless books, phone books, and a good selection of literature.
>
>> o Use verbal prompts frequently with falling writers to keep bringing home the connection between reading and writing. Here are some prompts to try at appropriate times:
>>
>> o "Use your two pointer fingers to frame the word *there* on that page. Now, move your fingers and show me *the* inside that word. Now, show me *her*, and now, *here*. Write *there*. Good. Now read it aloud. What words can you find in *there*? Erase it. Write it again. Read it. Erase it. You are there!"
>>
>> o "Read your sentence aloud to yourself. Does it make sense? What did you forget? Always read back what you write to see if makes sense."
>>
>> o "If this word is hand and this word is sand, write stand."
>>
>> o "Read this word: mouse. Now, write the word house. What do you notice?"
>>
>> o "Check this word. Does it look right to you? How can you check to make sure?"
>>
>> o "If you were reading your own writing, what else would you want to know?"
>>
>> o "Go back and reread it, pointing to each word. What's missing?"
>
> ➤ Have kids engage in reading around the room while also writing around the room.
> ➤ Label objects in the classroom for students to read, and as they read them, have them write the words on whiteboards or index cards.
> ➤ Use comic books as a way of connecting oral language with the written word. Then have students write their own conversations in the conversation bubbles.

> ➢ Have a small group of students write a Reader's Theater script for their favorite fairy tale. In order to perform it, they must read it back!

Once you program the reading and writing connection into your thinking, you will see falling writers doing the same. Remember, what they can write, they read. Let's do both!

30

Catch a Falling
Writer by . . .

Guiding Writers in Small-Group Instruction

Teaching children to read in small groups makes sense.
Teaching children to write in small groups also makes sense.

S mall-group instruction is one of the best ways we can differentiate instruction for individual students. Without it, we are teaching "to the middle" while hoping we engage the advanced as well as the struggling students. Much time has been spent on small-group instruction for reading, while writing instruction has often been left to occasional conferences or written feedback.

Falling writers need to be taught *how* to write. This is perhaps the most important point in this entire book. They must be taught *how* because they don't know how! So you can pull a small group (no more than three or four at one time) of struggling writers together and guide them as they write. The teacher's role here is critical if students are going to progress rapidly. Here are the most important things teachers can do to guide falling writers in a small-group instructional session:

> ➢ Have oral conversations with the group, or with individuals in the group, to generate ideas for writing. After a bunch of ideas have been offered, ask the question, "How can you write about it?" Their response to that is what they should write first. Then build from that point.
> ➢ Offer verbal prompts that will help writers use what they know to write something they don't know. Here are three verbal prompts you will probably use often:
>
>> ○ "Say the word aloud. What sounds do you hear? Write them down. Say it again. What else do you hear? Write down what you hear."
>> ○ "Now, that's a word you need to know by heart. Write it fast on this scrap paper. Write it again. Let's have a race. Ready, set, go! Write it again. Now, write it into your story."
>> ○ "Read it back. Does it make sense and look right?"
>
> ➢ Share the pen with individuals to keep their success levels high and frustration low. You might write parts of words that you don't expect them to know and let them add the beginning and ending sounds. You might add a phrase to get them going if they are stuck or offer an adjective to make the sentence more interesting. The main thing is to let the children know that you are right there; coaching, supporting, and encouraging them as they write.

Falling writers need prompting, modeling, and encouragement. They need to know what good writers do and how good writers solve problems as they write. They need to be taught how to generate ideas, edit their work, revise their writing, and publish their work. Small-group writing instruction is a way to move them forward, but it needs to be powerful and frequent.

Put your falling writers into the game, Coach! I invite you to join me in my lifelong quest to "catch them *all.*" My company slogan looks like this: Catch Them ALL."

Keep doing great things for kids and literacy!

Visit www.conniehebert.com, and write to me with questions or comments.

Appendix

Focus Sheets

U sers can personalize the sheets in this section by adding artwork or visual imagery that appeals to young writers.

FOCUS SHEET

Application

You have been hired by a famous bookstore to design a poster for this story. How would you advertise it?

FOCUS SHEET

Analysis

Write a letter to the author.

- Tell the author what you think.
- Ask the author three questions.

_____

_____

_____

_____

_____

_____

_____

_____

_____

_____

_____

_____

_____

_____

_____

_____

_____

_____

_____

FOCUS SHEET

Rate the Text

Too easy?	yes	no
Too hard?	yes	no
Interesting?	yes	no
Boring?	yes	no
Well written?	yes	no

FOCUS SHEET

Visualizing

Write or draw about something you could feel, taste, smell, see, or touch, in your mind, as you were reading:

FOCUS SHEET

Sequencing

What happened?

First: _____

_____

_____

_____

_____

_____

Next: _____

_____

_____

_____

_____

_____

Then: _____

_____

_____

_____

_____

_____

Last: _____

_____

_____

_____

_____

_____

FOCUS SHEET

Synthesis

Change the title of the story: _____

_____

_____

_____

_____

_____

_____

Change the setting of the story: _____

_____

_____

_____

_____

_____

Change two things that happened in the story: _____

_____

_____

_____

_____

_____

_____

What else could you change? _____

_____

_____

_____

_____

FOCUS SHEET

Evaluation

Draw or write about your *least* favorite part!

Recommended Web Sites, Research, and Texts

WEB SITES

Amazing incredible handwriting worksheet maker. www.handwriting worksheets.com

Busy teacher's café: A K–6 site for busy teachers like you! www.busy teacherscafe.com

Carl's corner: Resources and materials for classroom teachers, reading and resource specialists, speech therapists, parents, and students in the area of language arts. www.carlscorner.us.com

DLTK's sites: Growing together. DLTK's printable crafts for kids. www .dltk-kidscom

Don Johnston Incorporated. *Don Johnston: Access to learning.* www .donjohnston.com

Dr. Connie R. Hebert, national literacy speaker. www.conniehebert.com (author's Web site)

EdHelper: Math, reading comprehension, themes, lesson plans, and worksheets. www.edhelper.com

Family Education Network. *TeacherVision: Lesson plans, printables, and more.* www.teachervision.fen.com/teaching-methods/curriculum planning

Hubbard's cupboard: A Web site for early childhood educators and parents. www.hubbardscupboard.org

International Reading Association: The world's leading organization of literacy professionals. www.reading.org

Kurzweil Educational Systems: A Cambium learning technologies company. www.kurzweiledu.com

Macmillan/McGraw-Hill Companies education publishers: Building brighter futures. www.mhschool.com

Public Broadcasting System. *PBS kids.* www.pbskids.org

Reading A–Z: Your reading resource center. www.readinga-z.com

Starfall Education. *Starfall: Where children have fun learning to read!* www.starfall.com

WETA Public Television. *Reading rockets: Launching young readers.* www.readingrockets.org

RESEARCH

Armbruster, B. B., Lehr, F., & Osborn, J. (2003). *Put reading first: The research building blocks of reading instruction* (2nd ed.). Washington, DC: Partnership for Reading. Retrieved from www.nifl.gov/nifl/partnershipforreading/publications/PFRbooklet.pdf

Clay, M. M. (1972). *The early detection of reading difficulties.* Auckland, New Zealand: Heinemann.

Clay, M. M. (1993). *An observation survey of early literacy achievement.* Portsmouth, NH: Heinemann.

International Reading Association. (2000). *Excellent reading teachers: A position statement of the International Reading Association.* Newark, DE: Author.

Kameenui, E., Carnine, D., & Freschi, R. (1982). Effects of text construction and instructional procedures for teaching word meanings on comprehension and recall. *Reading Research Quarterly, 17*(3), 367–388.

National Reading Panel. (2000). *Teaching children to read: An evidence-based assessment of the scientific research literature on reading and its implications for reading instruction: Reports of the subgroups* (NIH Pub. No. 00-4754). Washington, DC: U.S. Department of Health and Human Services.

National Research Council. (1998). *Preventing reading difficulties in young children* (C. E. Snow, M. S. Burns, & P. Griffin, Eds.). Washington, DC: National Academy Press.

National Research Council. (1999). *Starting out right: A guide to promoting children's reading success* (M. S. Burns, P. Griffin, & C. E. Snow, Eds.). Washington, DC: National Academy Press.

Paris, S. G., Saarnio, D. A., & Cross, D. R. (1986). A metacognitive curriculum to promote children's reading and learning. *Australian Journal of Psychology, 38*(2), 107–123.

Pinnell, G. S., Lyons, C. A., DeFord, D. E., Bryk, A. S., & Seltzer, M. (1991). *Studying the effectiveness of early intervention approaches for first grade children having difficulty in reading* (Educational Report No. 16). Columbus: Ohio State University.

Stahl, S. A., Jacobson, M. G., Davis, C. E., & Davis, R. L. (1989, Winter). Prior knowledge and difficult vocabulary in the comprehension of unfamiliar text. *Reading Research Quarterly, 24,* 27–43.

Stiggins, R. J. (2001). The principal's leadership role in assessment. *NASSP Bulletin 85*(621), 13–26.

Stiggins, R. J. (2002). Assessment crisis: The absence of assessment for learning. *Phi Delta Kappan, 83*(10), 758–765.

Wu, H.-M., & Solman, R. T. (1993). Effective use of pictures as extra stimulus prompts. *British Journal of Educational Psychology, 63*(1), 144–160.

TEXTS

Reading Instruction

Bear, D., Invernizzi, M., Templeton, S., & Johnston, F. (2007). *Words their way: Word study for phonics, vocabulary, and spelling instruction* (4th ed.). Upper Saddle River, NJ: Prentice Hall.

Byrd, D., & Westfall, P. (2002). *Guided reading coaching tool.* Peterborough, NH: Crystal Springs.

Catts, H. W., & Kamhi, A. G. (2004). *Language and reading disabilities* (2nd ed.). Boston: Allyn & Bacon.

Clay, M. M. (1991). *Becoming literate: The construction of inner control.* Portsmouth, NH: Heinemann.

Cunningham, P. M. (2008). *Phonics they use: Words for reading and writing* (5th ed.). Boston: Allyn & Bacon.

Daniels, H. (2002). *Literature circles: Voice and choice in book clubs and reading groups* (2nd ed.). Portland, ME: Stenhouse.

Diaz-Rico, L. T., & Weed, K. Z. (2006). *The crosscultural language and academic development handbook: A complete K–12 reference guide* (3rd ed.). Boston: Allyn & Bacon.

Fink, R. (2006). *Why Jane and John couldn't read—and how they learned.* Newark, DE: International Reading Association.

Fountas, I. C., & Pinnell, G. S. (1996). *Guided reading: Good first teaching for all children.* Portsmouth, NH: Heinemann.

Fountas, I. C., & Pinnell, G. S. (1999). *Matching books to readers: Using leveled books in guided reading, K–3.* Portsmouth, NH: Heinemann.

Gentry, R. (1999). *The literacy map: Guiding children to where they need to be.* New York: Mondo.

Gillet, J., Temple, C., & Crawford, A. (2007). *Understanding reading problems: Assessment and instruction* (7th ed.). Boston: Allyn & Bacon.

Hebert, C. (2007). *Catch a falling reader* (2nd ed.). Thousand Oaks, CA: Corwin.

Heilman, A. W., Blair, T. R., & Rupley, W. H. (2001). *Principles and practices of teaching reading* (10th ed.). Upper Saddle River, NJ: Prentice Hall.

Mariotti, A. S., & Homan, S. P. (2005). *Linking reading assessment to instruction: An application worktext for elementary classroom teachers* (4th ed.). Mahwah, NJ: Lawrence Erlbaum.

McCarrier, A., Fountas, I. C., & Pinnell, G. S. (2000). *Interactive writing: How language and literacy come together, K–2.* Portsmouth, NH: Heinemann.

Opitz, M., & Ford, M. (2001). *Reaching readers: Flexible and innovative strategies for guided reading.* Portsmouth, NH: Heinemann.

Opitz, M., & Rasinski, T. (2000). *Good-bye round robin: 25 effective oral reading strategies.* Portsmouth, NH: Heinemann.

Tovani, C. (2000). *I read it, but I don't get it: Comprehension strategies for adolescent readers.* Portland, ME: Stenhouse.

Writing and Comprehension

Campbell, R. (2002). *Read-alouds with young children.* Newark, DE: International Reading Association.

Clyde, J. A., Barber, S., Hogue, S., Wasz, L. (2006). *Breakthrough to meaning: Helping your kids become better readers, writers, and thinkers.* Portsmouth, NH: Heinemann.

Dorn, L. (2001). *Scaffolding young writers: A writer's workshop approach.* Portland, ME: Stenhouse.

Feldgus, E., & Cardonick, I. (1999). *Kid writing: A systematic approach to phonics, journals, and writing workshop* (2nd ed.). DeSoto, TX: Wright Group.

Harvey, S., & Goudvis, A. (2007). *Strategies that work: Teaching comprehension for understanding and engagement* (2nd ed.). Portland, ME: Stenhouse.

Miller, D. (2002). *Reading with meaning: Teaching comprehension in the primary grades.* Portland, ME: Stenhouse.

Nettles, D. H. (2005). *Comprehensive literacy instruction in today's classrooms: The whole, the parts, and the heart.* Boston: Allyn & Bacon.

Pinnell, G. S., & Scharer, P. L. (2003). *Teaching for comprehension in reading: Grades K–2.* New York: Scholastic.

Rasinski, T. V. (2003). *The fluent reader: Oral reading strategies for building word recognition, fluency, and comprehension.* New York: Scholastic.

Short, K., & Harste, J. (with Burke, C.). (1995). *Creating classrooms for authors and inquirers* (2nd ed.). Portsmouth, NH: Heinemann.

Special Interest

Bracey, G. W. (2006). *Reading educational research: How to avoid getting statistically snookered.* Portsmouth, NH: Heinemann.

Charney, R. S. (2002). *Teaching children to care.* Portsmouth, NH: Heinemann.

Covey, S. R. (2005). *The 8th habit: From effectiveness to greatness.* New York: Free Press.

Diaz-Rico, L., & Weed, K. (2005). *The crosscultural, language, and academic development handbook: A complete K–12 reference guide* (3rd ed.). Boston: Allyn & Bacon.

Fang, Z. (2004). *Literacy teaching and learning: Current issues and trends.* Upper Saddle River, NJ: Prentice Hall.

Gardner, H. (2006). *Changing minds: The art and science of changing our own and other people's minds.* Boston: Harvard Business School Press.

Hebert, C. (2006). *Catch a falling teacher.* Philadelphia, PA: Xlibris Corporation. Available from www.xlibris.com

Jensen, E. (2005). *Teaching with the brain in mind* (2nd ed.). Alexandria, VA: Association for Supervision and Curriculum Development.

Strickland, D., & Alvermann, D. (Eds.). (2004). *Bridging the literacy achievement gap, Grades 4–12.* New York: Teachers College Press.

Tomlinson, C. A. (2001). *How to differentiate instruction in mixed-ability classrooms.* Alexandria, VA: Association for Supervision and Curriculum Development.

Tomlinson, C. A., & McTighe, J. (2006). *Integrating differentiated instruction and understanding by design.* Alexandria, VA: Association for Supervision and Curriculum Development.

Vygotsky, L. S. (1978). *Mind in society.* Cambridge, MA: Harvard University Press.

CORWIN

A SAGE Company

The Corwin logo—a raven striding across an open book—represents the union of courage and learning. Corwin is committed to improving education for all learners by publishing books and other professional development resources for those serving the field of PreK–12 education. By providing practical, hands-on materials, Corwin continues to carry out the promise of its motto: **"Helping Educators Do Their Work Better."**